SELECT COMMITTEE ON HOMELAND SECURITY

CHRIS COX, California, *Chairman*

JENNIFER DUNN, Washington, *Vice Chair*
C.W. "BILL" YOUNG, Florida
DON YOUNG, Alaska
F. JAMES SENSENBRENNER, Wisconsin
W.J. "BILLY" TAUZIN, Louisiana
DAVID DREIER, Calfornia
DUNCAN HUNTER, California
HAROLD ROGERS, Kentucky
SHERWOOD BOEHLERT, New York
LAMAR SMITH, Texas
CURT WELDON, Pennsylvania
CHRISTOPHER SHAYS, Connecticut
PORTER GOSS, Florida
DAVE CAMP, Michigan
LINCOLIN DIAZ-BALART, Florida
ROBERT W. GOODLATTE, Virginia
ERNEST ISTOOK, Oklahoma
PETER KING, New York
JOHN LINDER, Georgia
JOHN SHADEGG, Arizona
MARK SOUDER, Indiana
MAC THORNBERRY, Texas
JIM GIBBONS, Nevada
KAY GRANGER, Texas
PETE SESSIONS, Texas
JOHN SWEENEY, New York

JIM TURNER, Texas, *Ranking Member*
BENNIE G. THOMPSON, Mississippi
LORETTA SANCHEZ, California
EDWARD J. MARKEY, Massachusetts
NORMAN D. DICKS, Washington
BARNEY FRANK, Massachusetts
JANE HARMAN, California
BENJAMIN L. CARDIN, Maryland
LOUISE McINTOSH SLAUGHTER, New York
PETER A. DeFAZIO, Oregon
NITA M. LOWEY, New York
ROBERT E. ANDREWS, New Jersey
ELEANOR HOLMES NORTON, District of Columbia
ZOE LOFGREN, California
KAREN McCARTHY, Missouri
SHEILA JACKSON-LEE, Texas
DONNA M. CHRISTENSEN, Virgin Islands
BOB ETHERIDGE, North Carolina
CHARLES GONZALEZ, Texas
KEN LUCAS, Kentucky
JAMES R. LANGEVIN, Rhode Island
KENDRICK B. MEEK, Florida

JOHN GANNON, *Chief of Staff*
STEVEN CASH, *Minority Staff Director*

SUBCOMMITTEE ON INFRASTRUCTURE AND BORDER SECURITY

DAVE CAMP, Michigan, *Chairman*

KAY GRANGER, Texas, *Vice Cair*
JENNIFER DUNN, Washingotn
DON YOUNG, Alaska
DUNCAN HUNTER, California
LAMAR SMITH, Texas
LINCOLN DIAZ-BALART, Florida
ROBERT W. GOODLATTE, Virginia
ERNEST ISTOOK, Oklahoma
JOHN SHADEGG, Arizona
MARK SOUDER, Indiana
JOHN SWEENEY, New York
CHRIS COX, California, *ex officio*

LORETTA SANCHEZ, California
EDWARD J. MARKEY, Massachusetts
NORMAN D. DICKS, Washington
BARNEY FRANK, Massachusetts
BENJAMIN L. CARDIN, Maryland
LOUISE McINTOSH SLAUGHTER, New York
PETER A. DeFAZIO, Oregon
SHIELA JACKSON-LEE, Texas
BILL PASCRELL, Jr., New Jersey
CJARLES GONZALES, Texas
JIM TURNER, Texas, *ex officio*

IMPROVING SECURITY AND FACILITATING COMMERCE AT THE NORTHERN BORDER

JOINT HEARING

BEFORE THE

SUBCOMMITTEE ON CRIMINAL JUSTICE, DRUG POLICY AND HUMAN RESOURCES

OF THE

COMMITTEE ON GOVERNMENT REFORM

AND THE

SUBCOMMITTEE ON INFRASTRUCTURE AND BORDER SECURITY

OF THE

SELECT COMMITTEE ON HOMELAND SECURITY

HOUSE OF REPRESENTATIVES

ONE HUNDRED EIGHTH CONGRESS

FIRST SESSION

MAY 19, 2003

Committee on Government Reform

Serial No. 108–73

Select Committee on Homeland Security

Serial No. 108–4

Printed for the use of the Committees on Government Reform and Homeland Security

Available via the World Wide Web: http://www.gpo.gov/congress/house
http://www.house.gov/reform

U.S. GOVERNMENT PRINTING OFFICE

90–400 PDF WASHINGTON : 2004

For sale by the Superintendent of Documents, U.S. Government Printing Office
Internet: bookstore.gpo.gov Phone: toll free (866) 512–1800; DC area (202) 512–1800
Fax: (202) 512–2250 Mail: Stop SSOP, Washington, DC 20402–0001

COMMITTEE ON GOVERNMENT REFORM

DAN BURTON, Indiana, *Chairman*

BENJAMIN A. GILMAN, New York
CONSTANCE A. MORELLA, Maryland
CHRISTOPHER SHAYS, Connecticut
ILEANA ROS-LEHTINEN, Florida
JOHN M. McHUGH, New York
STEPHEN HORN, California
JOHN L. MICA, Florida
THOMAS M. DAVIS, Virginia
MARK E. SOUDER, Indiana
JOE SCARBOROUGH, Florida
STEVEN C. LaTOURETTE, Ohio
BOB BARR, Georgia
DAN MILLER, Florida
DOUG OSE, California
RON LEWIS, Kentucky
JO ANN DAVIS, Virginia
TODD RUSSELL PLATTS, Pennsylvania
DAVE WELDON, Florida
CHRIS CANNON, Utah
ADAM H. PUTNAM, Florida
C.L. "BUTCH" OTTER, Idaho
EDWARD L. SCHROCK, Virginia
——— ———

HENRY A. WAXMAN, California
TOM LANTOS, California
MAJOR R. OWENS, New York
EDOLPHUS TOWNS, New York
PAUL E. KANJORSKI, Pennsylvania
PATSY T. MINK, Hawaii
CAROLYN B. MALONEY, New York
ELEANOR HOLMES NORTON, Washington, DC
ELIJAH E. CUMMINGS, Maryland
DENNIS J. KUCINICH, Ohio
ROD R. BLAGOJEVICH, Illinois
DANNY K. DAVIS, Illinois
JOHN F. TIERNEY, Massachusetts
JIM TURNER, Texas
THOMAS H. ALLEN, Maine
JANICE D. SCHAKOWSKY, Illinois
WM. LACY CLAY, Missouri
———
——— ———

———
BERNARD SANDERS, Vermont (Independent)

KEVIN BINGER, *Staff Director*
DANIEL R. MOLL, *Deputy Staff Director*
JAMES C. WILSON, *Chief Counsel*
ROBERT A. BRIGGS, *Chief Clerk*
PHIL SCHILIRO, *Minority Staff Director*

SUBCOMMITTEE ON CRIMINAL JUSTICE, DRUG POLICY AND HUMAN RESOURCES

MARK E. SOUDER, Indiana, *Chairman*

NATHAN DEAL, Georgia
JOHN M. McHUGH, New York
JOHN L. MICA, Florida
DOUG OSE, California
JO ANN DAVIS, Virginia
EDWARD L. SCHROCK, Virginia
JOHN R. CARTER, Texas
MARSHA BLACKBURN, Tennessee

ELIJAH E. CUMMINGS, Maryland
DANNY K. DAVIS, Illinois
WM. LACY CLAY, Missouri
LINDA T. SANCHEZ, California
C.A. "DUTCH" RUPPERSBERGER, Maryland
ELEANOR HOLMES NORTON, District of Columbia
CHRIS BELL, Texas

EX OFFICIO

TOM DAVIS, Virginia

HENRY A. WAXMAN, California

CHRISTOPHER DONESA, *Staff Director*
NICK COLEMAN, *Professional Staff Member and Counsel*
NICOLE GARRETT, *Clerk*
JULIAN A. HAYWOOD, *Minority Professional Staff Member*

CONTENTS

IMPROVING SECURITY AND FACILITATING COMMERCE AT THE NORTHERN BORDER

MONDAY, MAY 19, 2003

HOUSE OF REPRESENTATIVES, SUBCOMMITTEE ON CRIMINAL JUSTICE, DRUG POLICY AND HUMAN RESOURCES, COMMITTEE ON GOVERNMENT REFORM, JOINT WITH THE SUBCOMMITTEE ON INFRASTRUCTURE AND BORDER SECURITY, SELECT COMMITTEE ON HOMELAND SECURITY,
Niagara Falls, NY.

The subcommittees met, pursuant to notice, at 9:30 a.m., in Festival Theater, Visitor Center, Niagara Falls State Park, Niagara Falls, NY, Hon. Mark E. Souder (chairman of the Subcommittee on Criminal Justice, Drug Policy and Human Resources) presiding.

Present: Representatives Souder, Camp, Shadegg, Sweeney, Sanchez, Slaughter, and Jackson Lee.

Also present: Representative Quinn.

Staff present: Christopher Donesa, staff director and chief counsel; Nick Coleman, professional staff and counsel; Mandy Bowers, professional staff member; and Nicole Garrett, clerk.

Mr. SOUDER. The subcommittee will come to order. And I'd like to yield for a brief welcome from Congresswoman Slaughter.

STATEMENT OF HON. LOUISE SLAUGHTER, A REPRESENTATIVE IN CONGRESS FROM THE STATE OF NEW YORK

Ms. SLAUGHTER. Thank you so much, Mark. I'm so pleased just to have this distinguished group in this area this morning. I can't prove this but I would think it would be most unlikely that we can find eight Members of Congress in one spot for a hearing. And so I'm double honored as they have come here to the northern border this morning. Now, you know who many of them are.

One of the nicest things that I love about this new district and I do love it, is getting to work with Jack Quinn and his office. That's always a delight and I'm happy to have Jack with us this morning. I'd like to introduce John Sweeney who is one of New York's most important Members of Congress. He's serves also on a Select Homeland Security Committee and he'S also on the Appropriations Committee. And it is of most delight that John is here he's very helpful to us in what we're trying to do for the State.

Dave Camp is from Michigan. And he is the chair of the Homeland Security Border and Infrastructure Subcommittee. And then you've met Mark Souder, who is the chair of the Government Reform subcommittee on Criminal Justice, Drug Policy and Human Resources and is our expert here this morning because he's been working on this issue long before the Select Committee on Homeland Security was even thought of.

On my right is Congresswoman Sheila Jackson-Lee from Houston. We've been working with Sheila for years on the southern border, we're delighted to have her here today to see the northern border and to work with us there. She is also a member of the Border Security and Infrastructure Subcommittee, so you'll have four group members of that subcommittee here today.

We have two more coming. We have Congressman John Shadegg from Arizona who chairs the Emergency Responders Subcommittee, Mark's committee. His plane is coming in and he will get here as soon as he can. And Congresswoman Loretta Sanchez, from California will also be arriving, and she is a ranking member on the Border and Infrastructure Committee and Select Committee.

I'm the ranking member on the Rules Committee, so I'm going to keep the rules, I guess. But in any case, I am so happy to have all of you here. First you got to see our majestic Seventh Wonder of the World, out here in the back and this is the best place to see it from. It is a great honor and I think the recognition as I said of Western New York's importance in our continued battle with terrorism.

And I am certainly pleased, I don't see where they've gone, but I have two MPs—there they are, they're still up top there. I'm delighted to have them here with us today. They have just traveled back from U.S.-Canada parliamentary meeting which is held annually for the last 44 years, it's been absolutely wonderful and they're our great friends and people who have our interest at heart as we have their's.

So I'd like to introduce Mr. Derek Lee and Mr. John Maloney and they will be testifying on our third panel. Welcome gentlemen. We're happy to have you here. And I want to recognize the men and women of Western New York here this morning. The Federal, State and local workers who are out there daily on the vigilant watch and we are grateful to you.

I was privileged to have the occasion last week to meet the committee of our first responders in the 28th District and I'm glad to have many of you here with us today. We acknowledge your commitment and your dedication. And you know last week certainly brought a sad reminder at the threat of terrorism in our allies. One of the cold blooded killers like those we saw on September 11th murdered once again, in the name of hate.

The State Department is now warning there are other soft targets around the world in danger. It's a real threat to our security that brings us here today. We may be thousands of miles away from Morocco and Saudi Arabia, but the terrorists persist. So we're here to talk about the things we can do to make sure we can be ready if anything does happen. As we sit around the great falls, it represents extraordinary power. There's also marks on the northern border and the huge vulnerability.

U.S.-Canadian border is 5,525 miles long, in some areas it's pretty remote. Securing it is not an easy task. Unlike the southern border, where we've poured resources into security for years, we considered security around the northern border less of a priority because it was not necessary. We're good friends with the Canadians, the fact that they are our largest trading partners, we know each other so well, it's never been any kind of threat at all on that border.

But it's possible that someone can come across this border. We can remember in 1999 just before the Millennium that alert Canadian border guards stopped a man coming through Washington State, whose stated purpose was to blow up L.A. Airport. So here we've got several points of entry from Canada, where we want to make sure while we are secure we are also able to continue our commerce and our easy movement back and forth across the border.

Lots of works is being done to make sure that we can do that. And we're right here in this area we have four international bridges, three international airports and two of the largest hydropower facilities in the world. It is terribly important for the rest of this country that we secure those assets and make sure that they are safe. So let me again thank all of my colleagues. I won't say they've come armed with an awful lot of information already and know that what we eat most here are chicken wings and beef-on-weck. And so we'll try to treat them to some of that before they leave today and go back to Washington. Thank you again for being here.

Mr. SOUDER. Thank you. Good morning and thank you all for coming. Today the Subcommittee on Criminal Justice, Drug Policy and Human Resources, which I chair, and the Subcommittee on Infrastructure and the Border, chaired by my friend and colleague Dave Camp, will explore the status of security and law enforcement along this section of the Canadian border. Since the summer of 2001, the Criminal Justice Subcommittee has been making a comprehensive study of our Nation's borders, focusing particular attention on the effectiveness of the Federal law enforcement agencies entrusted with protecting and administering the borders and ports of entry. Last summer my subcommittee released a comprehensive report on these issues, but our study continues.

In March and April of this year, my subcommittee held field hearings concerning the U.S.-Mexico border in Sells, AZ and El Paso, TX. Today, we return our focus to the northern border. We've already had hearings in Vermont and the Northeast part of New York State, as well as Washington State and multiple visits along the entire border. Today we return our focus here in upstate New York. U.S.-Canada border sees considerably less illegal activity than the southern border, but the nature of the illegal activity on the northern border raises special concerns.

First, the problem of cross-border drug smuggling is a serious and growing problem. In particular, I have deep concerns about moves by the Canadian Government to decriminalize marijuana, which has much the same practical effect as legalization. Such efforts will cause more problems at the border crossings, which will affect law enforcement, trade and travel. Much of the marijuana being smuggled out of Canada is not your typical marijuana; it is very high-potency, sometimes 4 and 5 times as much as 10 times, more similar in strength to cocaine or even heroin. This new marijuana often called "B.C. Bud" or "Quebec Gold" has been on the rise, and I hope that Canada will take this into consideration as it develops its new drug policies.

Other serious drug trafficking problems have been illegal smuggling of methamphetamine precursor chemicals through Canada, such as the cold medicine pseudoephedrine. It is of particular concern since many of the smugglers have been linked to Middle Eastern groups that may have ties to terrorists. The Canadian Government has begun the process of bringing some regulations to the precursor trade to which we're very thankful but more progress needs to be made.

The second significant danger we face here is the potential for terrorists to sneak across the northern border. In the Buffalo area, there are numerous avenues for potential terrorists to cross, and numerous tempting targets. There are four nuclear power plants on the shores of western New York State and many major bridges vital to cross-border trade and travel. The vulnerability of this area to this kind of attack was illustrated just last year, when the Federal Government announced the arrests of six Yemeni-American men described as an Al-Queda "sleeper cell" in the suburb of Lackawanna.

The U.S. Federal Government has responded to these vulnerabilities by doubling the number of border patrol agents in the Buffalo sector, adding customs and immigration inspectors at the local ports of entry, and expanding Coast Guard patrols of sensitive areas. New surveillance equipment and tightened border crossing regulations have also been added. Still, the northern border remains vulnerable to penetration. Moreover, the increased security at the legal ports of entrance threatens to slow commerce and hurt both the regional and the national economy unless it is implemented properly.

These issues are all very important and extremely urgent, and we look forward to hearing from our witnesses today about ways to address them. I first want to thank the personnel of Niagara Falls State Park for hosting this hearing today. I also when to thank Chairman Camp of the Border Security Subcommittee for agreeing to hold this hearing jointly with us, and for the assistance that he and his staff provided to us in setting it up. I am also a member of Mr. Camp's subcommittee, and I have appreciated his leadership on these issues. I further want to thank the ranking member of the Border Security Subcommittee, Mrs. Sanchez, who should be here shortly and my other colleagues from the House of Representatives for joining us as well.

We also welcome the representatives of the U.S. Federal agencies primarily responsible for dealing with border security and drug smuggling in this region. Namely the Department of Homeland Security's Bureau of Customs and Border Protection and the U.S. Coast Guard, and the Department of Justice's Drug Enforcement administration. My subcommittee is vitally interested in ensuring the effective functioning of these agencies, and we will continue to work with them and their staff to ensure the continued security and effective administration of our Nation's borders and its protection from narcotics. We welcome Mr. Michael D'Ambrosio, Interim Director of Field Operations at the Bureau of Customs and Border Protection's Buffalo Field Office; Commander Paul Gugg, Commanding Officer of the U.S. Coast Guard's Buffalo Marine Safety Office; Mr. Peter Moran, Chief Patrol Agent of the U.S. Border Patrol's Buffalo Sector; and Mr. William Walker, Associate Special Agent in Charge of the DEA's New York Field Division.

Border policy, of course, affects not simply the United States but also Canada. As such, it is of vital importance that we seek the input of our neighbors to the north in evaluating changes at the border. In each of our areas of the northern border we taxed Canadian parliamentarians as well as other representatives from Canada to make sure that we acknowledge their concerns in the trade questions between our countries, and this is pointed out by Mr. John Maloney and Mr. Derek Lee and they will be here. This past weekend I had the pleasure of attending the U.S.-Canada Interparliamentary Conference at Niagara-on-the-Lake, where I met with these gentlemen as well as many other officials of the Canadian parliament, we're glad that they are able to join us today.

When examining border policies, we must also seek the input of representatives of the local community whose lives are directly affected by changes at the border. Representing a law enforcement agency entrusted with protecting local citizens from drug smugglers and other cross-border criminals, we are pleased to be joined by Sheriff Thomas Beilein of the Niagara County Sheriff's Department. Mr. Kevin Feely, president of the local Chapter 154 of the National Treasury Employees Union will testify about working conditions for our inspectors at the ports of entry. Ms. Dawn Hamilton of the PBS affiliate WNED joins us to discuss ways to improve communication with first responders and other security personnel. Here to discuss the impact of international traffic on one of the most important bridges in the world is Mr. Stephen Mayer, who's the general manager for Operations for the Buffalo and Fort Erie Public Bridge Authority. We're also joined by two witnesses who can testify to the impact that border security policies have on the local economy and local businesses: Mr. Russell Deveso, chairman of the New York State Motor Trucking Association; and Dr. Andrew Rudnick, president of the Buffalo Niagara Partnership. We thank everyone for taking the time this morning to join us for this important hearing. And I'd now like to yield to Chairman Camp.

STATEMENT OF HON. DAVE CAMP, A REPRESENTATIVE IN CONGRESS FROM THE STATE OF MICHIGAN

Mr. CAMP. Well, thank you very much, Chairman Souder. As has been mentioned, the ranking member of this subcommittee is on her way here, Loretta Sanchez. This is a hearing that the Government Reform Committee had scheduled for some time. The Homeland Security Committee is a new committee and so I want to thank Chairman Souder for letting us join together to have a joint hearing with both the Criminal Justice Subcommittee of Government Reform and the Infrastructure and Border Security Subcommittee of Homeland Security Committee. It's a pleasure to be in Niagara Falls today. I want to thank Congresswoman Slaughter for letting us have this hearing in her district as well. I guess when I flew in I flew into Congressman Jack Quinn's district, so I'm learning the district lines in this part of thc country. The Buffalo Niagara border crossing ranks in the top three in total land border crossings in the Nation and is second only to Detroit in the amount of freight crossing in the northern border each year. Nationwide, border security has become a top priority and the Buffalo region is a perfect place to demonstrate what's being done on the northern border to improve security.

The potential scope of border security is immense. The challenge before us is to provide a level of security that's appropriate for the risks, including cargo screening, monitoring who and what is coming in and out of the country without hindering legitimate commerce and travel. I do not believe these are mutually exclusive goals.

Shutting down borders or delaying the flow of commerce in the event of a terrorist attack or in the name of increased security would have serious and longstanding effects on the national and world economy. This is especially true in communities like this, where "just-in-time" deliveries are essential to the local employers. The security and livelihood of the United States depends more than ever on how efficiently Federal agencies charged with border management achieve their respective missions and coordinate their functions.

During this hearing, I'm particularly interested in the flow and dissemination of crucial intelligence information from national headquarters to the field offices, as well as access to the FBI data and intelligence reports. As the chairman of the Subcommittee on Border and Infrastructure for the House Homeland Security Committee, I'm also interested in how technology is advancing the respective missions that we have before us.

Since September 11th, at the direction of the President, the top priority of the agencies like Customs, U.S. Border Patrol and Coast Guard has been responding to the continuing terrorist threat on our land borders, seaports and airports. These agencies are working diligently to protect our homeland by keeping terrorists and terrorists weapons from entering United States while enhancing our economic security by moving goods and people efficiently across the borders. As some of our witnesses today are working on the front lines to secure our borders, I'd like to thank them for their service and look forward to hearing their testimony as well.

I appreciate the members of the Canadian House of Commons testifying today. With almost $1.4 billion crossing our common border every day, an ongoing dialog and increased cooperation or harmonization, if you will, is essential to maintaining our strong security and economic relationship. I am also looking forward to hearing from community witnesses representing law enforcement, the private sector and other strategic areas that are involved in the security partnership.

I want to thank you all for being here. I want to thank my fellow members for being here. I've been in a lot of hearings in Washington and there were fewer Members in attendance as we have here today. So I think it's a real statement to how important these issues are and how much the Members do want to hear the information that may be discussed today. Thank you for being here. I look forward to your testimony. Now, I would yield to Congressman Sweeney.

STATEMENT OF HON. JOHN E. SWEENEY, A REPRESENTATIVE IN CONGRESS FROM THE STATE OF NEW YORK

Mr. SWEENEY. I thank you chairman and thank Chairman Souder for the invitation the opportunity to be here. As a fellow New Yorker I want to also recognize, acknowledge and thank my friend Louise Slaughter and my dear friend Jack Quinn for allowing an Easterner to come a little bit west to understand a little bit better the policies that effect us. I, Mr. Chairman, am not going to submit for the record a formal statement because I think it's quite important that we hear from the witnesses and I'm interested in the information that they have and they will share with us.

As a New Yorker I recognize the critical decisions that we're going to make in Washington and their application here on the border and the effect it has on the quality of life of the people that I represent in my district, both in terms of their safety and security and in terms of the economy of the region. I'm particularly interested to see how we have developed a system, how that system is working. And most particularly how the interaction between local, State and Federal agencies is occurring and what improvements and changes that we can make into that system, as well as ensuring that Federal resources reach where they need to reach.

As a member of the Appropriations Committee, we're right in the process of marking up the 2004 budget at this point in time so there are a lot of critical decisions that are gonna be made in the next several weeks and your testimony here in this panel and the following two panels testimony will have a real impact on policy as it's made in Washington. And I thank you for the opportunity to be here.

Mr. CAMP. Thank you. And I should have mentioned, the rules of the full committee apply here at this hearing and that means any Member who waives their opening statement has that time added on to their questioning time. But why don't I defer to Congresswoman Jackson Lee, if she has an opening statement you're welcome to make that now.

STATEMENT OF HON. SHEILA JACKSON-LEE, A REPRESENTATIVE IN CONGRESS FROM THE STATE OF TEXAS

Ms. JACKSON LEE. Thank you very much, Mr. Chairman. Let me first of all thank you for joining with Chairman Souder for this very important hearing. And to be able to be hosted so aptly and appropriately by Congresswoman Slaughter being in her district, I want to thank her particularly for her vision and leadership on these issues, along with my good friends Congressmen Sweeney and Quinn who are here as well and I look forward to my other colleagues joining us.

Mr. Chairman, I guess I'll be penalized, but I just have a brief few remarks and I'd ask that my entire statement be submitted into the record. I am grateful to be able to be in Niagara Falls. I've heard great explanations about it from two young people that I've got to know, my mother and father who honeymooned here. So it's good to be in this very beautiful area and I want to thank the community as well as the various panelists and witnesses that will be here. And particularly the members of parliament from Canada for your interest in this area.

This is a big border that is more than 5,000 miles long and certainly I've spent a lot of time coming from Texas on the southern border and seeing the lack of difficulty in moving across the southern border, even with the Rio Grande. It's important for us to be in this region because I have made the point of noting that there should be no second rate or second class border.

Just a few days ago we saw the tragedy of 19 individuals seeking to come into the United States losing their lives in a smuggling ring. It is worth noting that smuggling takes place everywhere. It may not be in the degree that we saw in Texas and on the border, but it happens. And if you smuggle people, you smuggle drugs and you launder money.

And so all of these are intertwined. And this hearing is extremely important so that we can get a sense of the need here on the northern border region. I believe one of the important focuses of this hearing or should be, is the idea of providing resources and support for our U.S. Customs agents, certainly the Coast Guard we have reinforced over the last fiscal year and Border Patrol agents.

I'm particularly interested in retention and professional development training, as well as for our legislation dealing with improved compensation and benefits. And I've worked on legislation along those lines. I'd be interested in hearing from our witnesses as to the needs in this area so that the attention can be brought to this border.

I'm particularly interested as well in an improved and enhanced communication system that will have the capacity for law enforcement agencies to communicate between State and Federal agencies but also internationally. I always believe that when Members of Congress are invited to the districts of leaders of our Congress, that we should be problem solvers. We hope that we can come and listen to your testimony and bring the kind of added support to this region, to ensure that all of America is made safe by having two secure borders; the northern and southern borders. With that, I yield the rest of my time.

Mr. CAMP. Thank you. Now, I'd like to recognize Congressman Jack Quinn.

STATEMENT OF HON. JACK QUINN, A REPRESENTATIVE IN CONGRESS FROM THE STATE OF NEW YORK

Mr. QUINN. Thank you, Mr. Chairman. And I am certainly this morning out of my committee assignment, out of my district and my constituents think out of my mind often, but pleased to be here nonetheless. And Louise, I echo your opening remarks for we're now neighbors, particularly in your Buffalo office, almost right across the street from each other and our staffs are getting along famously.

The seriousness of the discussion this morning, although I can't stay, I need to move back to Downtown Buffalo in just a few minutes. It is critically important because a lot of these solutions we need to remember have solutions where one size doesn't fit all. And so that some of our concerns on the northern border aren't the same as the southern border. Some of our concerns in other parts of the country might not match what we need to do here with our good friends from Canada; a relationship we have had for so, so many years.

So I'll waive an opening statement. Welcome everybody to my little corner of the district and thank Louise for her hospitality, as well as Sergeants Castromen and Sakowski here at the park. Thanks.

Mr. CAMP. Thank you very much. Chairman Souder.

Mr. SOUDER. I want to say for the official record we find that Congressman Quinn is very seldom out of his mind.

Mr. QUINN. Don't put it to a vote, Mr. Chairman, while I'm here. [Laughter.]

Mr. SOUDER. Before proceeding, I'd like to take care of a couple of procedural matters. First ask and consent that all Members have 5 legislative days to submit written statements and questions for the hearing record. That any answers to written questions provided by the witnesses, also to be included in the record. Without objection, so ordered. And unanimous consent that all Members present be permitted to participate in the hearing. Without objection, so ordered.

Now our standard approach in congressional protocol is that Government witnesses representing the administration testify first. So our first panel consists of these witnesses. Would the witnesses on the first panel please rise, raise your right hands, and I'll administer the oath. As an oversight committee it's our standard practice to ask all witnesses to testify under oath.

[Witnesses sworn.]

Mr. SOUDER. Let the record show that all the witnesses responded in the affirmative. The witnesses will now be recognized for opening statements. We ask all witnesses, summarize your testimony in 5 minutes. We'll insert your full statements into the record, in addition to any materials you'd like submitted and any other testimony that members have. The green light is not working, is that correct? So when the red comes up, it's like a fairly abrupt halt. Maybe we can do it like 4 minutes 30 seconds or something like that. So we're gonna start with Mr. D'Ambrosio on behalf of the Bureau of Customs and Border Protection. And thank you for coming back again, you've testified before.

STATEMENT OF MICHAEL D'AMBROSIO, INTERIM DIRECTOR FIELD OPERATIONS, BUFFALO, BUREAU OF CUSTOMS AND BORDER PROTECTION

Mr. D'AMBROSIO. Chairman Souder, Chairman Camp, members of the subcommittees. Thank you for the invitation to testify before you today. My name is Michael D'Ambrosio. I am the Interim Director, Field Operations for the Bureau of Customs and Border Protection, Buffalo Field Office. My responsibilities entail providing leadership for the legacy agencies of Customs, Immigration and Agriculture for all ports of entry in the State of New York with the exception of New York City.

On March 1, 2003, the U.S. Customs Service, U.S. Immigration and Naturalization Service, and the inspection functions of the Agriculture, Plant Health Inspection Service merged into CBP within the Department of Homeland Security, while the investigative functions of U.S. Customs and U.S. Immigration and Naturalization merged into the Bureau of Immigration and Customs Enforcement.

The collective goal of CBP is to prevent terrorists and their weapons from entering the United States while, at the same time, facilitate the flow of legitimate trade and travel while the traditional missions of the respective agencies continue to be observed, we now have one common mission that will serve to enhance security of our borders.

The CBP is the guardian of the borders of the United States of America—America's frontline of defense. Within the Buffalo Field Office we have approximately 1,000 officers, which include Inspectors, Canine Enforcement Officers, Commercial Officers and support staff, who are working ceaselessly to protect the American public. These officers ensure that all passengers and cargo entering or exiting the United States are doing so in compliance with the applicable laws and regulations and that they pose no terrorist threat. These laws and regulations are enforced by CBP officers in a judicious manner.

There are challenges along the Niagara frontier. CBP has the responsibilities at two bridges in Buffalo; the Peace Bridge and the International Bridge at BlackRock. In the Niagara Falls area CBP is responsible for international traffic at the Rainbow Bridge, the Whirlpool Bridge and the Lewiston Bridge.

In 2002, these bridges funneled nearly 1.2 million trucks, 7.3 million privately owned vehicles, 48,000 buses and 3,300 trains through CBP. Commercial carriers delivered nearly 2 million cargo releases to screen and process, netting the U.S. Treasury nearly $139 million in duties. Vehicle, bus, train and pedestrian traffic resulted in the inspection of 19 million travelers. Although an overwhelming majority of this passenger, vehicle and cargo traffic was processed and released by CBP in an expeditious manner, it also resulted in a large number of enforcement actions being taken by our officers. For example, CBP and ICE Officers made 197 narcotics seizures including over 6,000 pounds of marijuana, over 72,000 tabs of Ecstasy and 11,738,000 tabs of pseudoephedrine and 420 arrests. They seized over $6.6 million in undeclared currency, refused entry to over 48,000 aliens, expedited the removal of 200 aliens, and intercepted over 2,100 criminal aliens. Additionally, there were 30 cargo seizures totaling nearly $1 million in value.

During the past year CBP has received a significant increase in the resources that has allowed us to accomplish our work more effectively and efficiently. Inspectional staffing in the Port of Buffalo has increased roughly 100 percent. Additionally, facilitation programs jointly administered by CBP and Canadian authorities have been implemented to allow for expedited, yet highly secure, border processing of both travelers and commercial conveyances. High technology devices that enhance our ability to balance our facilitation and enforcement efforts have been added to many border locations, including the Buffalo area and the Niagara frontier. These technological systems have allowed CBP to create a layered enforcement strategy that requires a potential adversary to defeat a variety of complementing systems in order to be effective. Please allow me to elaborate on the equipment used in this highly effective enforcement strategy.

First would be the Radiation Portal Monitors [RPMs]. RPMs provide a means to screen cars, trucks or other conveyances for the presence of radioactive and nuclear material without inhibiting the flow of commerce or traffic. These systems are capable of detecting both gamma and neutron radiation emanating from both natural sources and nuclear materials.

Currently, there are five RPMs at the Buffalo Peace Bridge and four at the Lewiston Bridge cargo facilities providing 100 percent screening of all commercial trucks entering the Port of Buffalo and Niagara Falls.

Another device is the Radiation Isotope Identifier Device [RIID]. A RIID is a device that verifies whether a source of radiation is a possible threat or a medical commercial source of radiation. The RIID can be used both as a screening device to detect the presence of radiation and to perform the identification of radioactive isotopes that have been detected by other radiation detection equipment, such as the RMPs. Currently the Port of Buffalo/Niagara Falls has six RIIDs deployed.

There are additional technological issues that I could tell you about but my time is up. I'd like to thank you for this opportunity to testify. I would be happy to answer any questions that you have at this hearing.

Mr. SOUDER. Thank you. Thank you very much.

The record will have all those, we may have some followup questions that we'd like to get into the record.

Commander.

STATEMENT OF COMMANDER PAUL M. GUGG, COMMANDING OFFICER, MARINE SAFETY OFFICE, BUFFALO, NEW YORK, U.S. COAST GUARD

Mr. GUGG. Morning, Mr. Chairman, Mr. Chairman, distinguished members of the committee. I'm Commander Paul Gugg and I'm the Coast Guard Captain for the Port of Buffalo, NY, which includes the Buffalo/Niagara region, the Saint Lawrence Seaway, Rochester, NY, and Erie, PA. It's a pleasure to appear before you today to discuss the role of the Coast Guard in protecting our public and our critical infrastructure, while at the same time, ensuring the safe movement of goods and people across the international border.

As Captain of the Port, I'm responsible for an area that covers over 450 miles of shoreline from Massena, NY to the Ohio Pennsylvania line. This area is often referred to as the gateway to the Great Lakes, as all incoming vessels must pass through the Buffalo zone. In addition to Captain of the Port, I'm also the Federal On-Scene Coordinator for response to environmental disasters, the Officer in Charge of Marine Inspections for inspecting and certificating commercial freight and passenger vessels and, the Federal Maritime Security Coordinator, which makes me responsible for planning and coordination of ports and waterways security. All of these roles are relevant to the work of your subcommittees.

With me today is Commander Jeffrey Hammond, I hope he's still behind me. Commander Hammond is the Commander of the Coast Guard Group Buffalo. He oversees 10 multi-mission Coast Guard stations with 33 boats that conduct search and rescue and law enforcements over an operational area that extends from Massena, NY to Fairport, OH.

With regard to improving security and facilitating commerce in the Buffalo/Niagara region of the northern border, the Coast Guard's mission is three fold. First, as we are partners in CBP and ICE, excuse me—first our partners in CBP and ICE are very aware what efforts are stepped up in securing one area of motorists border crossing, other areas become more attractive. The Coast Guard has and must continue to patrol effectively by water, air and land the area between the bridges, as other agencies clamp down on drugs and illegal immigration at those portals.

Second, knowing that terrorists focus on economic and symbolic targets we need to continue to identify and reduce the vulnerability of critical infrastructures such as bridges and key economic facilities, from waterside and waterfront attacks. Both of these missions are relied heavily on close coordination with other DHS agencies, our former brother agency the DOT and local organizations. My written testimony highlights some of the multi-agency groups with which we participate in a cross-training and resource leveraging initiative that we have successfully engaged with Border Patrol.

Also noteworthy, is that in this region the Coast Guard's undertaking of law enforcement missions, such as drugs and migrant innervation, is complimentary to enhanced port security. The assets in mission hours implored to accomplish one are not inclusive of the other. As a recent example, in the Saint Lawrence region the Integrated Border Enforcement Team combined anti-terrorism law enforcement operations netted several drug seizures.

Last, we facilitate safe and efficient water borne trade and transportation as an alternative to highway checkpoints and enhancing in air pollution. A single ship can carry as much as 800 trucks. The ferry scheduled to commence operations between Rochester and Toronto next spring can carry as many people as 16 tour buses and a string of cars bumper to bumper more than one half mile long on each voyage. Meeting American's expectations with regards to security in commerce in addition to our other important missions, such as environmental protection and search and rescue is a challenge.

But with your continued strong support and by continuing to work smart and by leveraging other agencies capabilities, we will undoubtedly succeed. We appreciate your focused interest in the northern border and particularly the Buffalo/Niagara region and enjoy the opportunity to show your staff our waterfront and our latest equipment. Thank you.

Mr. SOUDER. Mr. Moran.

STATEMENT OF PETER MORAN, CHIEF PATROL AGENT, BUFFALO SECTOR, U.S. BORDER PATROL, BUREAU OF CUSTOMS AND BORDER PROTECTION

Mr. MORAN. Chairman Souder, Chairman Camp, distinguished committee members, I am very pleased to have the opportunity to appear before you today to discuss the operations and law enforcement initiatives by the Bureau of Customs and Border Protection, U.S. Border Patrol in Buffalo, NY.

My name is Peter Moran, and I am the Chief Patrol Agent for the Buffalo Sector of the U.S. Border Patrol. I would like to begin by giving you a brief overview of the Buffalo Sector. Buffalo Sector's area of responsibility encompasses 450 miles of international boundaries stretching from the Ohio-Pennsylvania line to the Saint Lawrence Seaway near Wellesley Island, NY. All 450 miles are comprised of water boundary.

The Buffalo Sector is located near New York State's second largest city and is responsible for patrolling the areas adjacent to Canada's largest city, Toronto. This corridor between Buffalo and Toronto is a major funneling point for traffic, both legitimate and illegitimate, destined for New York City and other points along the East Coast. To address this enforcement challenge, the Buffalo Sector has 82 agents assigned to four stations. These stations are located in Tonawanda, Niagara Falls, Fulton and Wellesley Island, NY.

Operationally, the Buffalo Sector accomplishes it's mission utilizing a variety of methods and equipment. Linewatch, or the physical observation by our agents of the international boundary, represents the primary function of the Sector's personnel. This is supplemented through boat patrol, traffic check and transportation check operations.

The marine environment poses unique and formidable challenges to law enforcement officials on both sides of the border, as it permits virtually unlimited access to the United States or Canada by visitors, both lawful and unlawful, who have access to a boat, raft or other watercraft. Traditional electronic intrusion devices, used with success in a land border environment, are of little utility in a marine setting. Visual observation of the water boundary itself, by an agent manning a stillwatch position on a riverbank, aided by binoculars and night vision equipment, was, until recently, the only method of surveillance available.

Now, thanks to the funding provided by the Congress, two Remote Video Surveillance Systems are in operation along the Niagara River with an additional two scheduled to be operational this summer. Funding for additional RVSS sites was included in the fiscal year 2003 budget. We expect those camera systems to be fully operational in fiscal year 2004.

Not withstanding the technological advances utilized in border enforcement today, the greatest tool available to law enforcement along the U.S.-Canadian border is the outstanding spirit of cooperation and mutual assistance which exists between law enforcement officers on both sides of our shared border—be they Federal, State, provincial, county or municipal.

Examples of such cooperative efforts are the numerous Integrated Border Enforcement Teams located along the entire northern border shared with Canada and the United States. Two such IBETs exist within the Buffalo Sector area; one along the Niagara frontier and one in the Thousand Islands area. Another example of cross-border cooperation is Project North Star, a bi-national multi-agency forum consisting of law enforcement agencies from Canada and the United States. Project North Star mandate, as stated in its by-laws is to enhance existing communication, cooperation and partnerships between Canadian and American law enforcement personnel. To provide a method for local, county, State, provincial and Federal law enforcement agencies and associations to voluntarily coordinate their efforts. And to promote the exchange of best practices in a more effective utilization of assets and resources.

Project North Star is governed by four international quad-chairs, representing United States and Canadian law enforcement agencies. I am the U.S. Federal quad-chair. Project North Star's headquarters is located in Cheektowaga, NY and is currently staffed by three Border Patrol Assistant Chief Patrol Agents under my direction. Discussions are currently under way with Canadian officials to assign Canadian officers to Project North Star.

Another example of the spirit of cooperation which exists here in the Buffalo area is the exceptionally close working relationship that has been developed between the U.S. Border Patrol and the U.S. Coast Guard. In the days immediately following September 11 it became apparent to the Buffalo Sector that we needed to expand our boat patrol duties to include year round operation. Having little experience in cold weather operations, we immediately contacted the Coast Guard for assistance.

The Coast Guard not only met our expectations but exceeded them. This cooperation evolved into a virtual twinning of our operations, which includes joint marine patrols, on-shore marine patrols and training. Furthermore, we are in the process of connecting the visual feed from our RVSS system with the Coast Guard and are funding a joint docking project at the Coast Guard's Station Niagara.

For the first time in our Nation's history, we have a single uniformed law enforcement agency at the borders working as one to secure America against the terrorist threat. Not withstanding the training, the cooperation, and the equipment sharing, the thread that binds our agencies was and continues to be, protecting and securing our Nations borders. Better security. Better enforcement. Better intelligence. As has been demonstrated here in Western New York, the achievement of a complete security of our international border is not to be viewed as a singular one-agency effort, but as a collaborative multi-agency effort. One team. One fight.

In conclusion, while operational challenges remain, I am confident that the continued support of Congress will help us meet these challenges and assure a safer homeland. I thank the committee for the opportunity to present this testimony today and I would be pleased to respond to any questions that the committee may have. Thank you.

Mr. CAMP. Thank you.

Mr. SOUDER. Mr. Walker.

I want to thank you too, Commander. We really appreciate the time you spent with all the staff yesterday going up and down the border, all the bridges out on the water, up in the air. It is immensely helpful as we do the reports.

STATEMENT OF WILLIAM WALKER, ASSOCIATE SPECIAL AGENT IN CHARGE, NEW YORK FIELD DIVISION, DRUG ENFORCEMENT ADMINISTRATION

Mr. WALKER. Morning Chairman Souder and Chairman Camp, distinguished committee members. I am William Walker, Associate

Special Agent In Charge of the Drug Enforcement Administration, New York Field Division. I'm pleased to appear before you to discuss the role of the DEA regarding the New York/Canadian border and drug trafficking.

I would like to thank each of the respective subcommittees for supporting the men and women of the DEA in our vital mission. DEA's office in upstate New York continues to support joint State, local, bi-national and international drug investigations, as well as intelligence sharing. DEA is exceedingly grateful for the outstanding cooperation and assistance that we receive from the Royal Canadian Mounted Police. The cooperative efforts of the RCMP were critical to the successful conclusions of a number of multi-agency counterdrug investigations.

DEA investigates drug trafficking originating from the Canadian border and in the upstate New York region primarily through our offices in Albany, Plattsburg, Buffalo, Rochester and Syracuse. There's a total of 41 special agents in upstate New York and 27 DEA task force offices.

The 428 miles of the New York/Canadian border, with 26 points of entry, is one of the most active borders in the country as well as a favorite conduit for drug traffickers. Three of the four largest cities in Canada-Toronto, Montreal and Ottawa are within 2 hours drive from New York ports of entry, resulting in extensive commercial and private traffic across the border.

In addition to the normal points of entry, drug traffickers take advantage of the Akwesasne/St. Regis Mohawk Indian Reservation. It bisects the New York/Canadian border and covers 14,000 acres of the U.S. side and 7,400 acres in Canada. This reservation is completely unprotected by BICE—Bureau of Investigation and Customs Enforcement—and is a haven for smuggling narcotics, illegal aliens and what.

The primary drug threat of the U.S.-Canadian border are marijuana, pseudoephedrine, club and predatory drugs and Southeast Asian Heroin. Highly sophisticated Canadian based drug trafficking organizations smuggle massive amounts of hydroponic marijuana across the border to New York State. The marijuana shipments are destined not only for the New York market but for further transshipment throughout the United States.

Hydroponic marijuana has become a major concern to the Drug Enforcement Administration because of the potency that you discussed earlier. This increased marijuana traffic is being actively pursued by DEA and is amplified by Operation Northern Comfort, which targets the distribution of hydroponic marijuana from Canada by members of the Hells Angels organization throughout the United States via the Mohawk Reservation. Approximately 34 defendants have been arrested to date and over $1 million seized in this ongoing investigation.

The illegal diversion of pseudoephedrine is also a particular concern to DEA in the upstate region. Pseudoephedrines is a precursor for methamphetamines and is continually diverted from legitimate to illegitimate sources for further transshipment, primarily to the West Coast. Canada based traffickers capitalize on the vulnerability of the border region as well as the one legal trade of pseudoephedrine in Canada, to facilitate the shipment of the drug into the United States. Pseudoephedrine, highly controlled in the United States, was not regulated in Canada until January 9, 2003.

Drug traffickers based in Canada also serve as a prominent source of supply for club and predatory drugs, especially GHB/GBL, Ecstasy and steroids. To counter this threat, DEA instituted Operation Webslinger; a ground breaking, multi-jurisdictional investigation which targeted the illegal Internet trafficking of "date rape" drugs. The DEA, together with several other U.S. agencies, the Royal Canadian Mounted Police and Ontario Provincial Police arrested over 115 individuals in 84 cities across the United States and Canada.

More importantly, we seized more than 1,500 gallons of GHB and GBL. Part of Operational Webslinger, DEA, Buffalo conducted the first court authorized contemporaneous interception of Internet Web sites. This led to the identification and arrest of a major Canadian citizen who was a significant supplier of club and predatory drugs. Intelligence and ongoing investigations indicate that multi-thousand pill quantities of Ecstasy are being smuggled from Europe through the Canadian border to New York along various points of the border.

Canada is a significant entry point of Southeast Asian Heroin as well. Southeast Asian Heroin organizations based in Canada receive and support shipments of heroin for further transshipment across the border into New York. DEA will continue to meet these challenges and these drug threats and is committed to intelligence sharing information and coordinating investigative initiatives to maximize counter drugs efforts along the border.

Thank you for this opportunity to appear before this subcommittee. I will be happy to answer any questions you or other Members will have.

Mr. CAMP. Thank you very much.

I want to thank all the witnesses for their testimony. I do want to acknowledge that Congressman John Shadegg from Arizona is now here. And, John, I'd like to give you the opportunity to make an opening statement if you wish or we can add that on to your question time.

Mr. SHADEGG. Mr. Chairman, I'll insert my opening statement into the record.

Mr. CAMP. Thank you very much. I just have a couple questions and then we'll go throughout the rest of the panel. But Commander Gugg, how are the Coast Guard operations being coordinated with the Border Patrol? I know we heard some testimony on that but particularly is there a clear line of communication between the different entities and do you have interoperable computer systems? And I just heard a little bit about the joint training, but can you tell us a little bit about how really the merging of these two different entities is going?

Mr. GUGG. Well, for one, Mr. Congressman, we're actually co-located in several areas; including Niagara. As you folks may have noticed the Border Patrol boat is right there at our station in Niagara. We talked about the cross-training so that we're using the same standard procedures. And something that's kind of ground breaking initiative is that we actually share frequencies with Border Patrol now. Each Federal agency typically has its own communication frequency and you've probably heard communication problems before where one can't talk to the other one. We believe we've overcome that to a large degree in the Buffalo area.

Mr. CAMP. And do you have data bases that interface with one another?

Mr. GUGG. We have a scheduled sharing type of data base, a calendar, but as far as a formal data base, sir, no we do not yet.

Mr. CAMP. And can you tell me how the mission of the Coast Guard might have changed as a result of the merging of the departments; particularly with regard to the entire Great Lakes? Because really we have vessels that enter the system and go throughout the Great Lakes Region.

Mr. GUGG. It hasn't changed too horribly much since the merging of the departments but since September 11 our emphasis focus—our focus has changed dramatically. The Homeland Security related things were always a mission of the Coast Guard but it was significantly less than 10 percent of our efforts and at times at least 60 percent of our efforts in recent months, sir.

Mr. CAMP. Mr. D'Ambrosio, the—again, I'm interested in the interoperable compatible computer systems and the use of electronic manifests for shippers prior to arrival at the border. And how can those systems be implemented and can you give me a little update on that?

Mr. D'AMBROSIO. Mr. Chairman, are you referring specifically to the 24 hour rule or something else?

Mr. CAMP. The 24 hour rule but I guess in general how new technologies can be brought on line to help keep our borders open to bring enhanced cross-border travel and commerce, while protecting security at the same time?

Mr. D'AMBROSIO. With regard to the Niagara frontier, I'll focus on that. It's a land water operation overwhelmingly. We currently do not have an automated manifest system for trucks. We do for rail. The automated manifest system for rail has been in effect for at least 4 years here at the border. There is a manifesting requirement that's going to be implemented under the Trade Promotion Act. The final rule I believe is due in October of this year. My expectation, based on discussions with headquarters, is that there will be something in place within a year for trucks to transmit electronically some period of time before arrival at the port of entry what is on the truck. The pieces of that electronic system have not been finalized yet.

The publication in the Federal registry has not taken place yet, so I really can't address it until that is published. But there is the intent to have an electronic system to know what's coming in a commercial conveyance; all forms of commercial conveyances in addition to the rail that we currently have.

Mr. CAMP. I'm aware of the press reports—first let me say in your testimony you mentioned the increase of resources that have been made available to the border. I'm aware of the press reports of the young boy who crossed undetected into the United States. Can you give me any new information that may not have appeared in the paper that can maybe sort of explain the situation and what steps may have been taken and how this could have happened?

Mr. D'AMBROSIO. Mr. Chairman, I don't know all of what happened because it's under investigation. It has been referred to our office in Internal Affairs. I understand the Inspector General is looking at the issue, so until we have all of the information from what occurred, it's hard to say how we would address it. Of course every inspector at the start of every shift, receives something called a muster. And in the muster we give them the latest intelligence information related to terrorism or narcotics smuggling, whatever it is. Of course it was reinforced after that event with every inspector that nobody enters the country without inspection. Now, if that did occur and under what circumstances did it occur, that will be shown in the investigation.

Mr. CAMP. All right. Thank you.

Congresswoman Slaughter, you care to inquire?

Ms. SLAUGHTER. Thank you very much. Mr. D'Ambrosio, I'm pretty much impressed by your testimony and the new equipment that you have in radiation form machines and radioactive isotope device and you're well supplied with those. It's more than adequate to what you think you'll need here.

Mr. D'AMBROSIO. Well, we will be receiving actually more RIIDs, the isotope detectors. We will be receiving more—and I'm speaking in terms of the entire area of my coverage, not just the Buffalo/Niagara frontier but all of New York State; the borders for New York and Canada. This is a work in progress. We will be receiving more radiation portals, more RIIDs. Some of the devices I did not get into, I don't know if you'd like me to address those now?

Ms. SLAUGHTER. I would.

Mr. D'AMBROSIO. OK. Each inspector wears a personal radiation device [PRD]. That personal radiation device will give a reading of gamma ray material that is near the inspector. A type of a first line of defense if a vehicle or conveyance has not come through a portal. The RIID is something that is used to verify after that initial alert, what might be there. The RIID is much more precise. It will also identify the isotope, where as the PRD will simply give a reading that something anomalus is in the presence of the inspector.

In addition to these radiation detector type devices, we have the VACIS, which is the Vehicle and Cargo Inspection System. That is a gamma ray system whereby an entire conveyance is run through this device. It sees into the conveyance and shows on a computer screen what is inside the conveyance. So the inspectors who are well trained, it's a 2-week training, are able to read the screens.

Ms. SLAUGHTER. Do you have those yet?

Mr. D'AMBROSIO. Yes, there's one at the Peace Bridge and one at the Lewiston Bridge.

Ms. SLAUGHTER. I understand I learned last week that reduces the amount of time in checking cargo from 8 hours to 2½ minutes, is that correct?

Mr. D'AMBROSIO. Yes. If a truck needed to be unloaded the old fashioned way, you can imagine a 43 foot truck could take all day perhaps. Now we can make a decision whether it's high risk or low risk based on any anomalies that might become visible to a trained inspector. It takes a minute to run that truck through the VACIS, so we can screen many more conveyances, commercial conveyances today and have a higher level of confidence that they are a low risk and not need to deband them as we have in the past.

Ms. SLAUGHTER. Do you also examine rail cars for their cargo?

Mr. D'AMBROSIO. We currently do not have any VACIS capability for rail, but that is being implemented.

Ms. SLAUGHTER. And planes?

Mr. D'AMBROSIO. Yes.

Ms. SLAUGHTER. I'm very pleased to hear that.

One other question that probably isn't in the high level of Homeland Security it may not rank as high but is terribly important to our constituents here, and that is the large number of recreational boaters who are constantly going back and forth between the United States and Canada. And I'm being told that with the new regulations that should the United States go to a orange alert that all U.S. boats have to be seen visibly face-to-face by either INS or Customs agents before they can go back to their home ports. Are you familiar with that?

Mr. D'AMBROSIO. Yes. During alert level orange all watercraft need to be inspected face-to-face. Now that we are in alert level yellow, that is not the case.

Ms. SLAUGHTER. But in an orange alert this summer, should that happen, what are all these boaters going to do? My feeling is that they may have to go as far as Rochester and Buffalo, this is my area here but there's many people that may have to go as far down as Alexandria Bay, is that correct?

Mr. D'AMBROSIO. They would have to go to a location where there would be inspectors available to inspect them.

Ms. SLAUGHTER. I think that's something we ought to take a look at. I believe that's a terrible bottle neck there. How do you feel about that Commander?

Mr. GUGG. I agree it would be a bottle neck. There are a number of measures, security measures that are—do have an affect on American citizens. We try everything we can to reduce those but those particular procedures have been set in place as necessary and appropriate.

Ms. SLAUGHTER. One other question on the new radiation devices. You don't need both Canadian devices and U.S. devices. Are you sharing the cost or sharing any information or research on those?

Mr. D'AMBROSIO. As far as I know and I am in frequent discussions with my counterpart in Fort Erie Ontario. I believe CCRA, Canada Custom Revenues Agency is receiving their own VACIS units. I'm not aware that they have any other radiation or any radiation detector devices.

Ms. SLAUGHTER. Is there any way we can work together to avoid duplication that would work very well and save us some resources and use the money for other resources?

Mr. D'AMBROSIO. One of the ways that we are exploring working together is in a concept known as an International Zone. That has been a topic of discussion in the accord process between the United States and Canada for a number of years. So if we did have International Zones with inspectors from both countries working together, then yes, there probably could be a significant savings on the technology.

Ms. SLAUGHTER. Do you have any particular feelings about that, pro or con, any of you; about that kind of International Zone?

Mr. D'AMBROSIO. Well, I personally was involved in the process but it's ongoing.

Ms. SLAUGHTER. Part of bringing that level of understanding between Mr. Manly and——

Mr. D'AMBROSIO. Right. There have been some issues related to the level of authority that each country would have in the International Zone. If the zone were entirely in Canada let's say, there's a question of how much authority U.S. Customs inspectors and Immigration inspectors, now CBP inspectors, would have in that International Zone and that's a topic of continuing discussion.

Ms. SLAUGHTER. Jurisdictional issues?

Mr. D'AMBROSIO. Yes.

Ms. SLAUGHTER. Thank you very much.

Mr. CAMP. Thank you. Congressman Sweeney.

Mr. SWEENEY. Thank you, Mr. Chairman. I want to thank all of the witnesses for being here and for what really is deeply informative testimony that will allow us to more specifically focus our energies and priorities. I serve on both Select and on Props Homeland. On Select I also serve as co-chair of the Intelligence Committee. There's an area and it relates to this interconnectivity issue and I'm gonna ask a couple questions about that in a minute.

But there's an area that I have some concern about. It is both concern in terms of our capacity in the Federal Government to quickly process our end of the responsibility and then also develop its protocols that will amply protect both agency sources and methods of information. And that is a notion of how many security clearances are available, how many are out there, how many are needed and how we are gonna develop a system to manage those clearances.

And I was—I suppose this is a question for both for the Commander and Mr. D'Ambrosio, but also you Mr. Moran in the sense that you're dealing both from the macroperspective and then also in the very front line of where those security issues are gonna really meet the greatest challenges.

Mr. D'Ambrosio, you mentioned that at the beginning of every report the teams on both border-crossing and the inspectors is what you called a muster report.

My question very simply is how many of your folks, you have 1,000 inspectors in the region, how many of your folks have that kind of security clearance that not only enable them to receive precise threat information in real time and then to whom are they able to transmit it to, in either the Commander under the Commander's control and Mr. Moran's control in order to react in real time?

Mr. D'AMBROSIO. Congressman, every inspector is cleared at least for information that is at the official use only level and that would generally be the level of the intelligence information that is given to them. The intelligence information frequently is the same information that has been in the newspapers. They would be informed of the kind of interdiction that took place let's say, on the southern border and maybe that technique may be applicable now to the northern border.

When you start to get into the Secret and Top Secret levels that does not extend to the inspectors. With regard to sharing of the information, the same information that would be available in a muster to the inspector at the beginning of their shift would be available also to Border Patrol Agents and——

Mr. SWEENEY. If I could interrupt. That is the official use level, correct?

Mr. D'AMBROSIO. Yes. It's the kind of information that really shouldn't be discussed with anybody except for within the organization, but it very well could be already in the public domain.

Mr. SWEENEY. Have you or one of the other committees of jurisdiction on the appropriations side, I guess, with commerce justice with the FBI—and I'm on treasury postals with treasury, so I have kind of an umbrella view of what's available and what we have developed out there. Have you been asked or do you have a plan to develop a proposal that would allow for the incorporation at some levels of your purview, clearances for Top Secret and/or at least Secret clearances from the Federal Government; and do you see the need for such?

Mr. D'AMBROSIO. At what level, Congressman?

Mr. SWEENEY. Whatever level in your organization. The fundamental question is, does someone closer to the ground have that clearance and have we undertaken any plan to develop that?

Mr. D'AMBROSIO. I'm not aware of any plan at this moment within the Office of Field Operations to expand the Secret and Top Secret levels. I can tell you right now that I currently have a Secret clearance and I am in the process of being cleared for Top Secret clearance. The Port Director and Chief Inspectors have Secret clearances. It generally does not go at a lower level than that.

Mr. SWEENEY. Very good. At what point do you anticipate that your clearance will be approved, your Top Secret clearance, do you know that?

Mr. D'AMBROSIO. I really don't know.

Mr. SWEENEY. The other issue is are we able to expedite those clearances quickly enough? And that will be answered by other folks and I appreciate that. Commander, do you want to address that issue?

Mr. GUGG. Thank you, sir. We have approximately 20 of our 300 people that have security clearances Secret or above. I believe that's satisfactory for getting—for shifting operations as we need to related to security changes and alerts. But we have—we're fully aware that it is a cumbersome system when a new employee or new individual does come on board, it takes some time. Fortunately our people within the Coast Guard are pretty good at working that system, but it is as we know cumbersome and does take some time.

Mr. SWEENEY. Mr. Moran.

Mr. MORAN. Approximately 10 individuals and 10 of our agents do on our staff have Top Secret and I have Top Secret. Our intelligence agents who are at the field level have Top Secret, the agents that Mr. D'Ambrosio already testified to official use. I'm confident that at least for the Buffalo Sector we have the clearance levels at all levels that are appropriate.

Mr. SWEENEY. Thank you. I want to address both the Commander and Mr. Moran with a followup question to Chairman

Camp's question. We talked about the interconnectability, you mentioned that you are on like systems as it relates to scheduling. How far away are we on like systems as it relates to other communicating shared information?

Mr. MORAN. Between us and the Coast Guard specifically, the communication was a big thing if you're going to work out in the field, you have to be able to speak to each other. We determined that in very short order in our operations. We were working on that prior to September 11 and of course we accelerated that process post September 11.

We don't share any other data bases other than the scheduling. We work together face-to-face on a daily basis. We ride in the same cars, we ride in the same boats. I can't think of any real data bases that perhaps we might need to share. I think if one did arise we would certainly work together and get access to those data bases.

Mr. GUGG. There is certainly one other piece of information, I wouldn't call it a data base but it regards imagery. And I'll leave that to Border Patrol to say how much they want to say about that.

Mr. MORAN. The Remote Video Surveillance System, the Coast Guard and the Border Patrol share the water boundaries, it's very difficult to patrol. It can only be done visually. We are providing a feed to the Coast Guard so they will be able to see on our monitors exactly what we're seeing.

Mr. SWEENEY. In terms of technology I think one of the greatest concerns that we have is the connectability in an appropriate fashion in real time and whether that—those decisions need to be made I would stress with each of you. Many of those goals are gonna happen with folks like you rather than folks back at CHS in Washington or Congress because you know the process essentially what's gonna work.

Let me ask two very quick questions. One, Mr. D'Ambrosio, in as much a statement as you can give for me, and I know Ms. Slaughter and Mr. Quinn will agree will benefit us in our efforts in Washington, you talked about the VACIS system significantly speeding up the flow of cargo and transportation traffic through the area. I've been one, I know Louise Slaughter has been, John McHugh and a number of us have been prior to September 11th, talking about the agent infrastructure its effects on traffic. So maybe you could address very briefly for us the kinds of challenges you see and possibly the needs to improve those, in terms of the bricks and mortar infrastructure that allow you to better do your job.

Mr. D'AMBROSIO. As far as bricks and mortar are concerned, Congressman, there is a program that's afoot to rebuild virtually every port of entry in my area of responsibility. Where the last hearing took place, Chairman Souder's subcommittee in Champlain, NY a couple of years ago, that major point port of entry is scheduled to be rebuilt over the next 2 years.

Not only is there an indoor fixed VACIS unit, the only one of its kind on the U.S.-Canada border, but they just received delivery of another mobile VACIS unit, the entire infrastructure is going to be rebuilt. So that major ports of entry are getting the focus thanks to——

Mr. SWEENEY. On a scale of one to five, I see the light on, I have one more really important question in terms of need, five being high need and the need for restructure, one through five, very quickly?

Mr. D'AMBROSIO. At many of the locations the need is a four, that are commercial centers, where commerce comes through and trucks are processed. We would need to rebuild those facilities.

Mr. SWEENEY. And I thank you for that. And Agent Walker, let me just briefly say thank you for your testimony in particular as it relates to the risks at the St. Regis—that are presented at the St. Regis Mohawk Indian Reservation and our ability to develop a coordinated multi-jurisdictional enforcement effort. Not just in drug interdiction but in terms of immigration issues and potential threats on the terrorists side. I've spoken to a number of both FBI and other law enforcement sources in upstate New York and in the region, and there is a great deal of concern in terms of our ability to develop a program. Mr. D'Ambrosio, you've mentioned it I'm sure. And with my time having run out, I'd like to followup at some other point with a more specific question about that. But if there are any comments that you'd like to quickly make but my time has run out. With that I'll thank the chairman for extending my time.

Mr. CAMP. Thank you. I would like to recognize that the ranking member of the Infrastructure and Border Security Subcommittee Congresswoman Sanchez has now arrived and I'll give her a minute to absorb some of the testimony. Why don't I now ask Congressman Jackson Lee if she'd like to inquire?

Ms. JACKSON LEE. Thank you, Mr. Chairman. I'm delighted to also be able to welcome the ranking member of our subcommittee. She's traveled a long distance and I'm delighted that she's here. The testimony has been very instructive and I want to pursue some of the lines of legislative action that I've been involved in. Let me, Mr. D'Ambrosio, speak to the question of your RPMs and congratulate you, as I understand your testimony suggests, that you've done 100 percent on commercial vehicles, is that accurate?

Mr. D'AMBROSIO. That's correct, Congresswoman.

Ms. JACKSON LEE. And that the—any commercial vehicles, any types whether it's a truck or any other type of vehicle that's involved in commerce, is that correct?

Mr. D'AMBROSIO. That's correct, that comes across at the Peace Bridge or the Lewiston Bridge.

Ms. JACKSON LEE. In so doing, what are you able to tell us in terms of what you're finding? Have you been able to intercept and stop illegal activities or have you found smuggling of human beings, drugs, etc.? What have you been able to determine out of this?

Mr. D'AMBROSIO. With regard to the RPMs, which detects radiation, we have not in my area of responsibilities yet found anything that would be related to a weapon of mass destruction. With regard to the smuggling of aliens, the VACIS, which shows images of what is inside of it, there have been in my area of responsibility the detection of aliens in commercial conveyances, detection of narcotics. So that the two together, the radiation detectors and the VACIS, which will indicate anomalies which are not related to radiation, provide a far stronger line of defense than we had just a year ago.

Ms. JACKSON LEE. So you're better able now with the combined equipment to really target in on problems that we might be having with respect to smuggling across the border.

Mr. D'AMBROSIO. Absolutely, yes.

Ms. JACKSON LEE. And Mr. Moran, you're on the ground. Mr. Walker, your responsibility is with DEA and as a member of this committee, I thank you very much, all of you for your service and for your testimony. And Mr. Gugg, obviously coming from Texas the Coast Guard is very prominent and we thank you for acknowledging the folks in the south, but we are gratified of your presence and the work you're doing. But let me focus in on the smuggling of persons and would all of you just respond to drug contraband. Are we seeing a better solving of problems or intercepting of the smuggling of aliens, with respect to either the new resources or the new focus? Mr. Moran.

Mr. MORAN. First of all, the Buffalo Sector, thanks to Congress, doubled in size over the past year. Those agents on the ground have made a significant difference. We have twice as many people out there this year as we had last year, that has translated into interception of more smuggling loads. Coupled with the RVS system, a system that is just beginning to be put into place but already with results. For example, the first day at one of the sites we apprehended 50 pounds of hydroponic marijuana coming across. We have literally saved the life of a smuggler who dumped his raft in the middle of the Niagara River. Along with the Coast Guard, we went out and plucked him out of the cold waters of the Niagara River. We intercepted smuggling those coming across the river. So the combination of the personnel plus the technology is making a real difference up here along the Canadian border.

Ms. JACKSON LEE. And is there a major problem of smuggling aliens in this region?

Mr. MORAN. The numbers cannot compare to the southern border. It is more organized along the U.S.-Canadian border. And it tends to move around much like as it does in the southern border. We make an impact in an area in Buffalo and they'll move to Detroit or up into Vermont.

Much like the southern border, the flow will move depending upon the threat that we pose to them. But we have noticed this fiscal year an increase in the smuggling of Costa Ricans. It's easier to get in to Canada. As a visitor, they come to Canada and then they get into the United States either through a port of entry hidden in a vehicle or in this area by raft, across the Niagara River. So we have seen an increase but nothing that compares with the numbers down south.

Ms. JACKSON LEE. And the culprits, perpetrators, are they—how would I say it, truckers in the normal course of commerce just taking an opportunity for easy money or are these people who are long time perpetrators of this criminal activity? I'm trying to find out the profile of the individuals that may be doing this, helping to smuggle; meaning the truckers or the vehicle persons bringing them across.

Mr. MORAN. I think that they run the whole range from an individual walking into a Canadian tire store on the other side and buying a $25 raft in the middle of the winter and paddling across, to a highly organized alien smuggling operation from Chinese—or you name the nationality, there's probably an organization dedicated to smuggling them. Anything related to a higher level of the smuggling organizations I would defer those questions to ICE, Immigration and Customs Enforcement Branch of Homeland Security. They deal with the investigations of those higher level groups.

Ms. JACKSON LEE. Let me quickly move and just ask—you mentioned that you doubled in size. I've been working on since coming to Congress a number of years on the retention, training, compensation for Border Patrol Agents. Have we improved over the years or can we do more in professional development training in height of the added responsibilities that you have? Maybe Mr. D'Ambrosio and both of you would like to answer that.

Mr. MORAN. From the Border Patrol perspective the attrition that is a problem along the southern border is not really a problem along the northern border. We do not except trainee agents up here on the Canadian border. The agents apply for positions that exist up here, so they're coming up here willingly versus being assigned. They're seasoned journeymen officers who have been in the Border Patrol at least several years before they ever come to work.

But the attrition is not the problem. I know the grade levels have been a problem for our agents. We have lost some to the Department of Transportation Security on the grade levels——

Ms. JACKSON LEE. So something along those lines to look at again would be helpful to you with respect to grade levels, compensation?

Mr. MORAN. That would be helpful.

Ms. JACKSON LEE. That would be helpful. What about professional development and training, enhanced training?

Mr. MORAN. The training we have is vigorous, both the academy training program. Some of that post September 11 was postponed as we were all forward deployed. And of course there's also now a merging of various branches within the Department of Homeland Security. I'm sure training functions will also be consolidated to give us more cross-training which will be needed.

Ms. JACKSON LEE. Mr. Walker, if you would, I'm curious and I would like to know about the St. Regis Mohawk Indian Reservation. Are you all handling that on your own or are you collaborating with other law enforcement agencies which might include the Border Patrol, on the work that you're doing on the reservation?

Mr. WALKER. We're working together with all the law enforcement agencies; principally the New York State Police. They're our primary partner on the reservation. They actually conduct law enforcement operations on the reservation. So the investigations we do conduct are principally with the New York State Police.

Ms. JACKSON LEE. And what would be the governmental entity to restore the police powers of the tribal police? You made a statement that you'd like to see the police powers of the tribal police restored. Who would make that decision?

Mr. WALKER. I'm not sure who would actually give them back the power to, I don't know if it's Congress but——

Ms. JACKSON LEE. But you're making the request?

Mr. WALKER. Yes.

Ms. JACKSON LEE. I think that we're somewhere involved and I just wanted to be clear that you're making the request and that would be helpful to your work?

Mr. WALKER. Yes. We'd have a point of contact. It's difficult to penetrate and infiltrate Indians, so we would need Indians to—New York State Police and DEA agents who are not Native American's, who are not familiar with the reservation, it's difficult for us to actually penetrate and conduct undercover operations.

Ms. JACKSON LEE. I certainly wouldn't want this hearing to suggest that we're targeting them, but what you're telling us is that area is a very vulnerable area?

Mr. WALKER. Yes, it is.

Ms. JACKSON LEE. And besides drug smuggling, other opportunities raise up because of the vulnerability of the area?

Mr. WALKER. Yes.

Ms. JACKSON LEE. I'll just finish on this note, if you gentlemen can respond to this. What are the, if you will, the processes that you put in place to ensure that as we secure this area, that we balance the concerns on civil liberties and prohibit or do not engage in what we have called racial profiling?

Mr. MORAN. It has never been the policy, Congresswoman, of racial profiling within the U.S. Border Patrol. Nothing really has changed post September 11. We're obviously at a heightened sense of awareness, out there looking for suspicious activity. We have noticed a substantial increase in citizens calling us, sometimes substantiated, sometimes not. But there has been very much an increase in citizen awareness of what is happening along the border, certainly along this border which is entirely different than the southern border where everybody knows where it is.

Up here, most individuals we don't think of it or we never did. It's a border that is a hard fast impediment to travel. Since September 11 we are noticing a great deal of increased citizen involvement in reporting suspicious activity along the waterways.

Ms. JACKSON LEE. Thank you, Mr. Chairman.

Just a note that this comes obviously pursuant to the Arab community and so I just wanted to raise the question to be assured that you're aware of it and that the work that is being done is done to secure us but also recognize those sensitivities.

Mr. CAMP. Thank you. Congressman Shadegg.

Mr. SHADEGG. Thank you, Mr. Chairman. Let me begin, Mr. Walker, with you. I want to begin by thanking you for what I consider to be excellent testimony on the issue of the drugs that cross our border and the problems they cause. I have been with Congressman Souder up and down the Arizona-Mexico border, which is—my home State is Arizona and we've been to Nogales and to several other places along that border. Most recently we were at Sells, AZ which is on the Tohono O'odham Indian Reservation. And so I want to focus some of my questioning—and we were looking there at drug crossings and looking at important efforts—we looked at the efforts then of both Customs and Border Patrol and DEA, along with the efforts of the tribal authorities in that area.

I want to focus a little bit on the Akwesasne St. Regis Mohawk Indian Reservation that you mentioned in your testimony. The first question I have is—and you just reiterated it, apparently here in

New York State, law enforcement has jurisdiction on that Indian reservation?

Mr. WALKER. The New York State Police patrol—they're on the—that's the only law enforcement we work with primarily is the New York State Police.

Mr. SHADEGG. And they would have jurisdiction within the boundaries of the reservation?

Mr. WALKER. Yes.

Mr. SHADEGG. That makes it somewhat unique in that in Arizona at least that I know of where local law enforcement has no jurisdiction. One of the—some of the testimony we heard when we were in Sells, AZ on the Tohono O'odham and quite frankly this has now been picked up by the major newspapers in Arizona since then, is that the burden imposed upon the reservation itself, both on law enforcement agencies of the tribe trying to deal with drug interdiction and on environmental damage by crossers, has caused a huge financial burden for the reservation. Have you heard comments by this reservation by this indian tribe, with regard to the burden imposed upon them to control their—either for drugs or for other types of smuggling across the border?

Mr. WALKER. No, sir, I haven't, but we can get back to you on that.

Mr. SHADEGG. Mr. D'Ambrosio or Mr. Moran, do your agencies interdict drugs or interdict the flow of traffic of individuals that cross that indian reservation?

Mr. D'AMBROSIO. Congressman, the Office of Field Operations which I'm responsible, has authority only at the ports of entry. The Akwesasne Indian Reservation is between the port of Massena and Fort Covington. And that has been handled by a combination of what's now ICE and Border Patrol and State Police.

Mr. SHADEGG. Mr. Moran, do you have a comment?

Mr. MORAN. The Akwesasne Reservation is not in the Buffalo Sector's area, our area ends over by the Thousand Islands. So I would have to refer any questions specifically regarding the Akwesasne to the Swanton Sector of the Border Patrol.

Mr. SHADEGG. OK. Then, let me go back to you, Mr. Walker. I would appreciate very much if in addition to looking into the issue of the burden imposed on the reservation and the tribe itself, the other issue that came up with when we were in Sells, was the exploitation of tribal members by smugglers. The Tohono O'odham Reservation in southern Arizona on the border is vastly different than this. Mark and I were there, we flew over in a Custom's Black Hawk, there are places you can't tell where the border is because it's just raw desert and then three strands of barbed wire fence that was once there is gone.

But one of the issues that we were made aware of is and it has been gotten more press attention is exploitation of local residents in these remote locations by smugglers; come in and simply bribe them to help get drugs or people across the border. So I would appreciate if you would look into that issue as well as and get back to me on that.

Mr. WALKER. We certainly will.

Mr. SHADEGG. You would have only drug authority with regard to traffic across the border and then I guess none of the gentlemen here have authority here for other types of smuggling across that border, including the smuggling of terrorists across the border inside the reservation, is that right?

Mr. D'AMBROSIO. Right.

Mr. SHADEGG. Let me turn then to Mr. D'Ambrosio and Mr. Moran. I think, Mr. Moran, it was in your testimony that—the reference to the Remote Video Surveillance System that you currently have in place, is that right?

Mr. MORAN. That's correct, Congressman.

Mr. SHADEGG. And you've had those up and running for now—some of them for 2 years?

Mr. MORAN. A year.

Mr. SHADEGG. A year. Congressman Souder and I have been, as I said, on the Arizona-Mexico border. We are looking at various ways to patrol that border. Right now it's done by truck, it's done by ATVs, it's done by horseback, it's done by helicopter and it's done by these raised platforms, where people get up on the top of them and actually have a mechanical platform that goes up in the air and looks.

Can you describe for me the Remote Video Surveillance System you have; what distance they have and how they perform and whether you're happy with them?

Mr. MORAN. The systems we have now are a combination of thermal imaging device and a high resolution color television camera. They can see as far as the human eye can see. As far as actual tactical use, it's several miles, sometimes even more. They're particularly useful in the water environment since the water environment has to be done visually, the seismic sensors and infrared sensors don't——

Mr. SHADEGG. Nothing interferes with line of sight, you don't have trees or gullies or——

Mr. MORAN. Yeah, trees do present a problem up here along the border. We have to be able to get up above the trees in order to see the water. And it is very heavily populated which also presents unique difficulties.

Mr. SHADEGG. Are they faced just looking in one direction down the border, period, or are they remotely controlled?

Mr. MORAN. They can be controlled. They have I believe about a 340 degree radius, depending upon the situation. We also have mobile systems very similar to those that are for thermal imaging devices as well as infrared that are mobile.

Mr. SHADEGG. And their night capability is equal to their day capabilities as a result of the infrared?

Mr. MORAN. Yes.

Mr. SHADEGG. Have you looked at—one of the things that we're looking at in the southern border of the United States is the issue of—the Arizona Delegation recently turned in a letter requesting that unmanned arial of vehicles be funded on the southern border as a way to try to give us a better view of that border, which is a very, very long and very, very unprotected border. Have you looked at that as a possibility?

Mr. MORAN. The Border Patrol just recently received a rotary ring aircraft which has been a great help. As far as utilities, UAVs in this area, I guess I'd have to refer to the FAA. We have Toronto with the airports just across the river and of course the Buffalo/Niagara Region. I think a UAV up in the skies certainly in the Buffalo area. The Niagara frontier might pose problems with other commercial and military aircraft out of the airbase here in Niagara Falls.

Mr. SHADEGG. Those issues have been raised in the southern border as well, although we probably don't have the same degree of air traffic with the Luke Air Force Bombing Range portion of the Arizona-Mexico border and there is an issue of the Air Force in using that. There is a proposal, I think Chairman Souder has been working on that's creating a corridor along the border where UAVs could be flown in there, flown at lower altitudes, perhaps if you all want to come down and take a look at them, they cost a lot less than rotary aircraft to operate.

Let me ask both you and Mr. D'Ambrosio. There was testimony in your testimony about the coordination between your office and the Coast Guard and the fact that you now have radio frequencies that are the same. I guess having just heard Mr. D'Ambrosio refer to the fact that he has the ports and you have the rest of the border, I guess part of my question is how do you each feel about the degree of cooperation and interoperability that you have as we move forward into an integrated homeland security system and integrated border surveillance system?

Mr. MORAN. The ports and the Border Patrol have always had radio communication with each other. We have always worked very closely with the ports of entry. We respond to run throughs at the port of entry that we cover, we have a longstanding close working relationship.

Mr. SHADEGG. You were previously Border Patrol, correct?

Mr. MORAN. Still am.

Mr. SHADEGG. And Mr. D'Ambrosio, you're Customs?

Mr. D'AMBROSIO. Was Customs, now Customs and Border Protection, correct. I'd like to state that the Border Patrol has worked closely for years here at the U.S.-Canada border at the ports of entry. The only other law enforcement personnel is a Border Patrolman, so if there was a problem at the port of entry, the inspector is on the radio to the Border Patrol.

Mr. SHADEGG. Is there anything in Congress we can do in particular, with regard to the law—the new law, the Homeland Security Act and its merging of responsibilities or anything that we can do outside of the law, in terms of resources that would be of particular help to you in integrating that to a greater degree along with the Coast Guard?

Mr. D'AMBROSIO. At the moment I can't think of anything. I know that our radio contact has been on the front burner. In the northeast part of the State we have a little problem being worked on, not a resource problem, we just need to get a digital system in place. Offhand, I can't think of anything at the moment.

Mr. SHADEGG. Mr. Moran.

Mr. MORAN. I would agree with Mr. D'Ambrosio and I'm not aware of any problems in our resources.

Mr. SHADEGG. Thank you.

Mr. CAMP. Thank you very much. Congresswoman Sanchez, glad you're here, you may inquire.

STATEMENT OF HON. LORETTA SANCHEZ, A REPRESENTATIVE IN CONGRESS FROM THE STATE OF CALIFORNIA

Ms. SANCHEZ. Thank you very much, Mr. Chairman, and thank you for holding this hearing today. Sorry I came in late, I actually came from the San Diego area, you can imagine it's probably the furthest point one would come from. I am from southern California and am very aware of the southern border that we have and some of the problems we're having there. And since I grew up along the border, I really have seen the changes going on and how it effects our commerce, etc. So I'm very interested to hear from you with respect to what's going on with our northern border.

I guess the real question I asked myself when I take a look at what the Homeland Security Committee is trying to do, can the U.S. land borders really be secured to prevent infiltration of terrorists and instruments of terrorism; and that is the real question we have to ask ourselves. And my colleague from Arizona mentioned the Mexican-U.S. Border, which is under 2,000 miles, whereas I look at the Canadian border with the United States and it's 5,500 miles.

And, you know, when I look at the mission to monitor all of our borders in order to detect illegal intrusions and intercept and apprehend smuggled goods and people attempting to enter illegally, I think to myself managing the flow of people and goods to border check points is really only one aspect of what we're assigned to do now.

I have several questions and forgive me, I also did not get to read your written testimony because unfortunately Fed-Ex had thunderstorms through Memphis on Friday and Saturday, I'm sure my package with your information will arrive at my home today. But I'm here, I think it's important to be here, so here are my questions. And since I didn't know who would address them, pick and choose as you see fit.

What is the progress of implementation of the U.S.-Canadian Smart Border Declaration including the 30 points action plan? Is the Border Patrol properly equipped to accomplish this mission and can we improve in any way the State and Federal cooperation in these efforts? And last, because I get this asked all the time, I also sit on the Arm Services Committee, is there any role for the Department of Defense in border surveillance missions, is it a proper role—I'm not talking about the whole issue we have on the southern border where we have—I'm talking about the issue of border surveillance and how we take a look at terrorists or instruments of terror crossing our border?

Mr. D'AMBROSIO. Congresswoman, I guess I will go first and then pass it on to Mr. Gugg and Mr. Moran. With regard to the Smart Border, there are some aspects of it that apply to the ports of entry, I'll address those. We have implemented along the border—I'll focus just on my area of responsibilities which is New York State, a program called FAST. FAST is a way to identify low risk commercial transactions whereby the driver is cleared very thoroughly, background checked. The importer belongs to the Custom-Trade Partnership Against Terrorism. Again, enrollment is a commitment and specific commitment to making sure that supply chain is clean. He knows who his suppliers are, he knows all the routes of travel of his goods, and that the carrier is also on C–TPAT. It does the same thing that's been in effect now since early winter here at the Peace Bridge and at the Lewiston Bridge, it also is in effect at Detroit.

What FAST will do is it will give us a high level of confidence that those transactions present a very low level of risk. On a sample basis we'll verify that the risk is low for the most part of those commercial transactions without the need for the usual thorough check that those receive.

Ms. SANCHEZ. How many do you have signed up in this area?

Mr. D'AMBROSIO. Roughly 400. In addition to FAST, there's NEXUS. Now NEXUS is something equivalent which applies to privately owned vehicles and just pleasure travelers. We have a number of people—a few thousand that have signed up in this area, another few thousand—quite a few thousand in the Detroit Port Huron area. It will be expanding to Champlain, NY by mid summer so the major border crossings have Nexus in place.

That's a system whereby people have their background thoroughly checked. They carry a card with them. If the inspector is able to verify based on the photo of the person that appears based on an electronic transmission of the data to a card, to the computer screen, the people in the car have indeed been cleared for NEXUS. So these systems are in place and they're being expanded. We see the fruits of the resources that you have devoted to these types of things occurring, so that we have a more secure border but don't slow down legitimate travelers. We're able to provide devoted lanes to these low risk transactions. This kind of traffic can flow across smoothly. Anyone who doesn't participate is probably going to spend some time at the border.

Ms. SANCHEZ. I notice that not having the NEXUS card crossing the border Saturday night took me back 2½ hours versus probably 20 minutes.

Mr. D'AMBROSIO. I will pass it to Mr. Gugg.

Mr. GUGG. Sure. The Coast Guard doesn't have a huge role in the border—we do have frequent persons in our area who carry NEXUS cards, and what might seem of a quick fix to your question, that card entitles the bearer only to cross, so you can't have additional persons on that vessel that is not necessarily cleared for that. That's all I have.

Mr. MORAN. Congresswoman, with regard to the equipment and resources, again, I don't know if you were here but the Buffalo Sector doubled in size over the past year. We're anticipating an additional number of resources, I don't know exactly how many. We are funded for an additional 14 RVS which will give us a good handle on the Niagara frontier, good visuals on the Niagara River.

With regard to the State and local cooperation, it's been my been experience on the Canadian border since 1979, we have always worked very closely, not just with the State, the county and the municipal U.S. agents, but also with the Canadians. The list of traffic goes both ways. The criminals will go whichever way there's money, it's a two-way street. We're all working very closely. Of course we're trying to get even better at what we do but it's nothing new, since September 11 it's certainly ongoing. But since my time in 1979 it's been a daily function of law enforcement.

Ms. SANCHEZ. So with respect to monitoring all illegal intrusions and intercepting and apprehending smuggled goods and people, are you telling me that you're properly equipped to accomplish that mission at this point?

Mr. MORAN. As far as intercepting all, I don't know if that would be a realistic goal in our country.

Ms. SANCHEZ. That's in your statement, it says monitor all to detect illegal intrusions and apprehend people attempting to——

Mr. MORAN. The great challenge obviously would be to monitor all of the border, in-between the ports and that is a very large chore. Obviously that is a plausible goal and that is what we are working forward to achieve. The resources that you have given us are making an impact. As the resources come we will be able to make a greater impact along securing the border.

Ms. SANCHEZ. Again, are you properly equipped at this point?

Mr. MORAN. At this point within the Buffalo Sector we do not have the resources to guarantee the entire 450 miles of water boundary.

Ms. SANCHEZ. OK. Thank you. Back to the surveillance and the Department of Defense, do any of you have a comment with respect to that?

Mr. MORAN. The Border Patrol in the past has received some support mission from the Department of Defense, no surveillance missions. They have assisted us with intelligence analysts, radio technicians, that sort of thing. I do not see a need for militarization or active surveillance role for the military certainly in my area.

Ms. SANCHEZ. Any of you other gentlemen have any comment to that question?

Mr. GUGG. The Department of Defense technical support working group with regard to technologies is helping us evaluate the possible use of a portal rail detection at some of our check points for commercial vessels that pass. But again, that's limited to the technical support at this time.

Ms. SANCHEZ. With respect to expertise you all carry, would you say there is no role with respect to border surveillance, you should be doing it or it's already being done; and there should be no role for the Department of Defense? I'm just asking because as a member of the Defense Committee, we get asked all the time to put our military forces on the border for different reasons; one being this whole issue of surveillance. Personally, I prefer not to.

I'm just asking you as the experts who deal on a day-to-day basis, is a there a role for them or do you think the role falls under you and you have the resources and get the resources that you'd be able to do it?

Mr. MORAN. I continue to see a continued need for support. The military has equipment and expertise and expensive equipment that might not be cost effective for our Buffalo Sector to have this specialized equipment. I see a continued need for support operations, I do not see a need for law enforcement missions from the military.

Ms. SANCHEZ. Any others?

Mr. D'AMBROSIO. Congresswoman, at the ports of entry I don't see a role for the military. I would say the ports of entry are adequately covered by the staff we have in place.

Mr. CAMP. Thank you very much. Before we go to Chairman Souder, you have two other questions——

[Brief interruption.]

Mr. SWEENEY. This is borne out of questions asked by Mr. Shadegg and Ms. Sanchez, and I think it points out a level of concern that we have in terms of the interconnectability. And the question is to Mr. D'Ambrosio. You stated in your testimony that your responsibility entails providing leadership for the legacy agency for Customs, Immigration.

For all ports of entry in the State of New York with the exception of New York City, all ports of entry being waterports, being—what is a port of entry?

Mr. D'AMBROSIO. There are specified ports of entry designated by Congress. And they're the ones—Buffalo, Niagara Falls, Alexandria Bay, but also includes Albany, Syracuse, Rochester. But specifically relative to the inland ports, it would be the airports. In Rochester, right now there's the airport, but within a year there is development of a fast ferry coming in from Toronto. So it's evolving. It depends on where the commerce and where the modes of transportation come in. So Rochester would become then a seaport.

Mr. SHADEGG. This is my question, Mr. Moran has indicated in a question by Mr. Shadegg that the Buffalo Sector is a 450 mile stretch that does not include the St. Regis Reservation. Mr. Walker in his testimony said that therefore it is possible for an individual to legally enter the Canadian portion of the reservation and transit into the United States, without supervision.

You don't have supervisory capacity, you don't have supervisory capacity. There is an entity that oversees as it relates to the transportation of illegal entries, beyond interdiction, drug interdiction. There isn't anybody here who has jurisdiction over that. And my suspicion is there isn't anybody here on the northern border in New York much less the northern border period, that has that kind of specific oversight.

Is that your understanding as well? You have no authority by virtue of Act of Congress is what you're telling us today?

Mr. D'AMBROSIO. Over what, Congressman?

Mr. SWEENEY. Over the St. Regis Reservation.

Mr. D'AMBROSIO. That's correct.

Mr. SWEENEY. Because it's not designated specifically, you have no authority because it's another sector of the Border Patrol that has that authority?

Mr. MORAN. That's correct, Congressman.

Mr. SWEENEY. And there isn't any entity that you know of that has that kind of authority that connects you each up to the issues attendant to the transportation of illegal immigrants into the Nation through the reservation?

Mr. D'AMBROSIO. May I ask whether my colleague Mr. Peter Smith sitting in the back bench might have something to add to that? He's with the Bureau of Immigration and Customs Enforcement.

Mr. SOUDER. Mr. Smith, do you have anything you want to add? Will you raise your right hand?

[Witness sworn.]

Mr. SOUDER. It's Peter Smith?

Mr. SMITH. Peter J. Smith.

Mr. SOUDER. Thank you. State your rank.

STATEMENT OF PETER J. SMITH, SPECIAL AGENT IN CHARGE, BUREAU OF IMMIGRATION AND CUSTOMS ENFORCEMENT

Mr. SMITH. I'm Special Agent in Charge of the Bureau of Immigration and Customs Enforcement. Congressman, on that point there, what we do on the reservation, we work jointly. We've got 10 people, special agents assigned to the Massena office. We work closely and jointly with the DEA, the Border Patrol and the New York State Police to enforce the customs laws along the reservation. It is a very political issue. We safeguard the intelligence going back and forth and our enforcement actions that we do. But when we do them, we do them jointly and together.

Mr. SWEENEY. How great is your capacity? I don't want to belabor the point, we can do some followup on it. How successful and how much of a concern is the reservation and your capacity with those multi-agencies?

Mr. SMITH. The biggest concern that we've had in the last 18 months has been the money going up to Canada, illegally through the reservation and the that's marijuana coming down through Canada through the reservation and getting into New York State.

Mr. SWEENEY. I thank you, Mr. Smith. Let me ask one question that's sort of connected with it, the FBI set up 56 car terrorist task forces throughout the country, I believe there's one in western New York. Is that not true? It is true. Are any of you members of that task force or are all of you?

Mr. GUGG. Yes.

Mr. SWEENEY. Coast Guard is. DEA?

Mr. WALKER. DEA is.

Mr. D'AMBROSIO. Office of Field Operations is not.

Mr. SWEENEY. Do you know if there is any reason for that, has that been explained?

Mr. D'AMBROSIO. Again, we're very operational, very port specific. And again, I would think that Mr. Smith, who is a member of that unit and we work closely with what is now called——

Mr. SWEENEY. So essentially there are two customs units?

Mr. D'AMBROSIO. Well, there were. Now they're two separate bureaus.

Mr. SWEENEY. All right. I will followup and I thank you.

Mr. MORAN. The Border Patrol also has a presence on that task force.

Mr. SOUDER. Thank you. Congresswoman Slaughter?

Ms. SLAUGHTER. Thank you, Mr. Chairman. I'm going to be very brief. I was very impressed in your testimony. I thank you for being here. I learned a great deal this morning and feel somewhat better about what's going on at the borders. One question though that I need to ask you is the question of first responders. I know you mentioned that you work very well with county government and other governments. Do you—do any kinds of—what is the chain of command of how you would get ahold of the fire chief or the police department, is that considered to be a problem of the local government; or do you have any sharing of information at all with the people that have jobs on the ground of keeping us safe in our houses when the border is breached or when we have reason to believe something is going to happen within the border?

Mr. MORAN. Congresswoman, if I may, the Border Patrol is a mobile uniform force between the ports of entry. We're out patrolling the roads all the time. It frequently happens that we will come across an accident, a fire or something along those lines. We have direct communications with the State authorities. We just get on our car radios and advise the appropriate authorities as to what——

Ms. SLAUGHTER. But if you thought it was a breach of security or something has happened that you were to get the information, despite all your best efforts and everything you have, something was probably going to happen in Buffalo let's say, you would have the ability immediately or some way to contact the people that would be necessary on the ground to be able to help you deal with that, they're not left out of this are they?

Mr. GUGG. I believe that would be best coordinated with the Joint Terrorist Task Force and the FBI, they practice this all the time and they have communication in place, it's a 24 hour watch.

Ms. SLAUGHTER. The FBI is not anywhere around the homeland security nor is the CIA, is that correct? So that means that what you do on the border itself and the coast, does not directly connect directly with the first responders?

Mr. MORAN. The Border Patrol does maintain a 24 hour a day, 7 day a week, 365 day a year communication factor. We have direct communication link with the State of New York and with the counties. There is a New York State Counter Terrorist Network that we have access to, and it's both ways. They can also contact us directly and we can immediately get it down to our people on the ground. They would do the same through their network. But it would be the communications centers that jump from Federal to State and county, that's where we make the jump. We advise the State, the State goes to their people and it works in the opposite direction.

Ms. SLAUGHTER. Well, I certainly hope that communication is fast enough and adequate, so we can get the information to the people who are going to be responsible, riding in our neighborhoods. We're all very impressed here with what happened with the Lackawanna Six, the interdiction of those people and the prosecution which certainly was a combination of what was done by the local responders and the FBI, as I understand it.

And so I wanted to be assured as I work with my constituents and the volunteer firemen who work hard, train so hard, the EMTs, that when something happens that's going to require their attention they are notified at once and considered to be partners in what you're doing.

Mr. CAMP. Thank you. And now I will recognize Chairman Souder. And again, I want to thank you for allowing us to have this joint hearing which really is an attempt to have the authorities as divided in Congress come together in a way that the statute requires. Chairman Souder.

Mr. SOUDER. First, I'd just like to point out for the record that it's been really interesting because some people work the north border and some people have worked the south border and there are just dramatic differences. Have any of you served on the south border? Why don't you say, what's the biggest difference you see here from the south border?

Mr. MORAN. It's colder. [Laughter.]

The volume. I was in a small station in Fort Hancock, TX, that little station apprehended about 10,000 people a year, there were 7 of us. So the volume down on the southern border is overwhelming. Up here I think you see more sophistication, it can be equally as dangerous to cross this border. Up here we've lost people attempting to cross the Niagara River. We've had in recent years a woman lose her leg riding a freight train across. So the dangers are there. Whether it's the southern border or northern border. But I say that the biggest single thing obviously is the numbers.

Mr. SOUDER. I want to put a couple things in the record to illustrate the numbers point. While we were having a hearing in Sells, AZ, there were four busts during the hearing that totaled 1,500 pounds of marijuana. In El Paso a couple weeks ago, when we held the hearing there, they have no prison base to hold anyone under 100 pounds. That is dramatically different.

Second, we held a hearing a few years ago where we heard from the DEA that when he was attempting to apprehend somebody, was shot at by the Mexican Police. And generally speaking on the north border the Canadian Mounties are not shooting at you. What we've had is the IBET teams, the CPATs, other things that you've talked about here, that is really a different type of border situation.

In parts of the southern border we're starting to get that cooperation and that's where it works best then where we don't have as much cooperation. The number of illegal immigrants is substantially less coming across the north than the south. You could walk all day and probably not see anyone trying to cross illegally to the open eye. But every single crossing I've been in California in-between the crossings, and Arizona and Texas, you can see people preparing to move across the border.

There's a substantially different type of challenge we have at the north border. But you also heard new things coming out of Congress, and the word is "all", which is kind of an unnerving word for the north border. It's unnerving in the north harbor where 16 members have said, can you assure that every package that's not contained to customs, does not contain any nuclear part; every package.

All are probably achievable but are more than just a vague goal, we're moving very aggressively because the type of things that we're looking at now compared to immigration and drugs, are catastrophic. Therefore, the questions as the terrorists become more sophisticated and we have reason to believe based on the experience we're seeing, that the north border in fact is more vulnerable right now in the question of terrorism than the south border.

So you're kind of seeing us in evolution just as your departments are in evolution, in trying to figure out resources, distribution and the demands on you are different. At the same time I want to ask a few questions in narcotics in particular because we're seeing some rising pressures on the north border. I have a couple questions I want to make sure we get in for the record.

First, on the Century NEXUS, Mr. D'Ambrosio, in the year 2000 the Department of Justice report said that there had been no time savings on NEXUS on the north border and that it had been minimal at best. On the south border we see dedicated lanes at San Isidro, at El Paso, at Lorigo and Magallan, but in the north is the primary reason that the studies have shown that it hasn't had a dramatic reduction. First off, has that changed in the last 2 years; and second, is it predominantly a problem of lanes on the bridges because of the water?

Mr. D'AMBROSIO. Mr. Chairman, my understanding of SENTRI which was a legacy immigration system was that there wasn't the level of participation in SENTRI since there was a charge for it. It was not as well used as NEXUS is becoming. NEXUS in an era of tighter security is viewed I believe by travelers is the way to get quickly across the border.

Mr. SOUDER. That was pre September 11, the study was?

Mr. D'AMBROSIO. Right. I can say here in Buffalo where there's the Peace Bridge and it's only three lanes. People will get through the procedures more quickly with a NEXUS card once they get across the bridge, once they get into the area where they can open up into these various lanes. But getting across the bridge in the middle of summer at the peak of traffic is still gonna be——

Mr. SOUDER. Which is a very critical point. That when we study time, we need to study the time that the Homeland Security is doing with their systems, not the wait time at the bridge because that's a separate question, if we don't have adequate bridges to cross. Because we control the number of ports of entry, so we can expand that. That's a huge problem in Windsor because even if we expand the ports of entry, they can't get more trucks across fast enough. So some of the studies will show there hasn't been a reduction in time, when in fact it's another problem, that is a infrastructure question.

I was just talking with the MPs from New Brunswick and they have a 3-hour wait at the main border which is nothing compared to San Isidro, but it backs up because you don't have enough ports of entry and you don't have enough bridges and there's not much you can do about it. Could you give us, for the record, if you don't know it right now, what percentage of commercial trucks you anticipate will be enrolled in the system?

Mr. D'AMBROSIO. Commercial trucks enrolled in FAST?

Mr. SOUDER. Yes.

Mr. D'AMBROSIO. The aim is to have at least 50 percent of the trucks enrolled in FAST.

Mr. SOUDER. What is it currently?

Mr. D'AMBROSIO. Currently? I can get that information.

Mr. SOUDER. Also, like a tracking of how you foresee that. That's for the whole Buffalo border?

Mr. D'AMBROSIO. Actually, it's for all commercial centers on the U.S.-Canada border.

Mr. SOUDER. We'd like the data for your border.

Mr. D'AMBROSIO. OK.

Mr. SOUDER. Can you explain the process the FBI, CIA, those intelligence agencies are not part of homeland security. How does that information, if you have somebody you've intercepted who is—you have questions about, let's say in-between the ports of entry, do you have—you have Top Security clearance. But is there a method and also at the ports of entry, are we proceeding to where that data even if you're an agent who is picking them up, does not have access to specific data, gets a pop-up or mark that this person is on a watch list? Do we have that sort of implement? Are you confident that if you intercept somebody in-between a crossing or at a port that the information we have elsewhere on our system that information will flag that individual?

Mr. MORAN. I could not speak to the specifics on what they would be inputting into our systems. We have a number of systems that we run every individual. But if we have any suspicion, Mr. Chairman, that's when we contact the Anti-terrorism Task Force which has access to all terrorists related systems. If there's any doubt in our minds, we routinely contact them. If we're done with them for instance and ready to let them go, we contact them to make sure they might not have some interest before.

Mr. SOUDER. That's any illegal that you might——

Mr. D'AMBROSIO. That would raise suspicions that they might possibility be involved or have any knowledge regarding, for instance, any terrorist activity would automatically be referred to the Anti-terrorism Task Force.

Mr. SOUDER. How would you decide whether or not that person is suspicious and must be checked out?

Mr. D'AMBROSIO. It might be something they have—every individual we apprehend is already run through a number of ours, and of course now, the Customs data bases. So if they were interested in somebody, it would automatically flag up when we ran them through our system.

Mr. SOUDER. So if someone has a passport from a nation that is a terrorist nation, would that be a flag?

Mr. D'AMBROSIO. I believe our current policy is if someone's from a nation that is seen as sponsoring terrorism, that is an automatic flag that a special interest alien would be run.

Mr. SOUDER. Mr. Smith, could you address the intelligence question?

Mr. SMITH. Yes. Information that is provided by the JTTF would come in to the Bureau of Immigration Customs Enforcement through a special agent we have assigned to them. When we get that information, we put it into the tech system and it goes nation wide. When the people are stopped, the Bureau of Immigration Custom Enforcement will go out and interview these individuals and start the process of obtaining and gaining more intelligence.

Mr. SOUDER. Thank you. I also wanted to ask Mr. Walker a few questions on the narcotics. You testified that you felt there was a stockpiling of heroin in Canada as well as in the United States, Asian heroin.

Mr. WALKER. Yes, we believe so.

Mr. SOUDER. Large stockpiling, small, do some signs of these—I think at least your written testimony you said you believe that to some degree there's been a somewhat decline in the usages? In other words, there's an oversupply coming out of Southeast Asia essentially into the U.S. market as that Colombian in Mexico?

Mr. WALKER. We believe that the competition between Colombian heroin and Southeast Asian heroin is going to come back full circle. Southeast Asian heroin we're seeing more of it, our complex monitoring program we typically only confront Colombian heroin. But there's an ongoing investigation that just hit the news yesterday that talks about our successful efforts with China, Southeast Asian heroin has always been a problem. We believe organizations based in Canada have stock piled heroin and are bringing it across the border.

Mr. SOUDER. On a couple of visits to Vancouver and also a hearing at the Blaine Border, what we heard was that the BC Buds, supposedly this high grade marijuana which literally sells for more than cocaine and heroin in my home town, and my understanding, New York City and Boston, that the heroin and cocaine or particularly cocaine are going north but there's a little bit, really Asian heroin was only in the northwest. Are you suggesting that some of that Asian heroin is now making its way across Canada and in the United States from Asia, coming down to this side as well?

Mr. WALKER. That is what our ongoing investigation and intelligence tells us, yes, sir.

Mr. SOUDER. That—do you see an interconnection between those who are dealing with the hydroponic marijuana and the heroin, cocaine, are they swapping, is there money going back and forth between those groups or are they different distribution groups?

Mr. WALKER. I don't think so. Let me ask the Assistant Special Agent In Charge. No, we haven't.

Mr. SOUDER. Now, my staff just told me that yesterday Customs informed them that hydroponic marijuana seizures were up 100 percent this year?

Mr. WALKER. Yes.

Mr. SOUDER. Are those—is much of that coming through Buffalo/Niagara?

Mr. WALKER. Yes. We seen an increase in Buffalo but as we were talking earlier, we don't know if that's a combination of increased assets on the border. We believe that the threat has always been there. We're getting more of it because we have more resources.

Mr. SOUDER. Could you do in the Customs at the ports of entry, I believe at Niagara was one of the places where you were doing back checking, going back into Canada. What are you finding from either Canadians who visit the United States, U.S. citizens or others, what are they taking back to Canada and has that program of interception found much?

Mr. D'AMBROSIO. That's what we call the out bound program which has found quite a few hundred thousand dollars in undeclared currency. Peter Smith could probably speak to this as far as investigations are concerned but really it's narcotics. Also interestingly we have found marijuana going to Canada, inexplicable, buyers would be going to Canada from the United States and coming in from Canada from the United States.

Mr. SOUDER. Colombian-Mexican marijuana?

Mr. D'AMBROSIO. I don't know what kind.

Mr. WALKER. I don't know.

Mr. SOUDER. Do you know, Mr. Smith?

Mr. SMITH. Yes, sir, it's Mexican.

Mr. SOUDER. So while in the west and in the Vermont, NY, Champlain corridor clearly that is coming down from Quebec, Canadian marijuana. The west is Vancouver, B.C., but in the middle we may be having less traffickers going up reverse direction. Let me—would you see that increasing if they change the laws on marijuana?

Mr. WALKER. It definitely would reduce risk by 50 percent. The risk would only be on one side of the border.

Mr. SOUDER. Let me ask a couple other questions. Are you still doing the out bound program?

Mr. D'AMBROSIO. Mr. Chairman, it's what we would call a program that we do when we have the opportunity. We have to judge whether it's going to cause excessive backups into neighborhoods, especially in the Buffalo area. We had been doing it after September 11th 24 hours a day, 7 days a week. We received a number of complaints that this was backing traffic up going into Canada. And we since refined it so that we will confine these operations at different times of the day unpredictability, in order to intercept mainly the currency exiting the country.

Mr. SOUDER. I would strongly suggest anybody who's even been at San Isidro and seen all the watchers on the border, that if the standard is when there's backups you don't check, that's when the high risk will move. That's the challenge we've got with the whole thing. Congresswoman Sanchez.

Ms. SANCHEZ. Mr. Chairman, with all due respect, I just wanted to not leave for the record an impression that I think that you left. And that is—and especially as the only Mexican-American here at this hearing, anecdotal situations shouldn't be implied with respect to a larger universe. I think it's not right for us to leave on the record that in some way or another that Mexican law enforcement is not working or is working against us.

I personally have a cousin who is very higher up in anti-narcotics, contra-narcotics in Mexico who has been shot 14 times at the border working with our American law enforcement who stop drug trafficking and others. So I think it's wrong to leave the impression in the record and also to the members here in the audience, that somehow or another something that may have happened at a hearing or during a hearing that you were having is sort of an implication that our Mexican counterparts are not working hard on this whole issue of drug and migration flow.

Mr. SOUDER. If I in any way implied that even a majority of law enforcement officers on the south border weren't committed, because the fact is there is greater danger, it's more complex. However, we do have more problems in some of the provinces and in fact, those like your relative who have tried to stand up have frequently been threatened. And I believe the current administration in Mexico, we have some areas there where now for the first time we're getting good cooperation but that doesn't mean individuals aren't constantly being threatened. The drug czars from Mexico were leasing an apartment that was controlled by the cartel. On the other hand there were other drug czars there whose lives were constantly threatened and it is more of a different challenge.

Ms. SANCHEZ. It is challenging but I would remind the chairman that in any group there are bad apples and I'm sure we could find them on the Canadian side and we could also find them in law enforcement in our own agencies in the United States. So just not to leave the impression for that comment. Thank you.

Mr. CAMP. Thank you. I want to thank the panel very much for their services and their testimony this morning. Thank you very much.

Mr. CAMP. I think we'll move to panel two. We have two members of Parliament, the Canadian House of Commons. The Honorable Derek Lee and the Honorable John Maloney.

Mr. SOUDER. I thank both of you for joining us here. We know you've both been very active for a number of years with the parliamentary group. Thank you for your testimony. Mr. John Maloney is from right across from Buffalo and I know it's very appreciated by his American colleagues for this work on the border issues and I look forward to hearing your testimony.

STATEMENT OF JOHN MALONEY, MEMBER OF PARLIAMENT, HOUSE OF COMMONS, CANADA

Mr. MALONEY. Thank you, Chairman Souder, Chairman Camp, Members of the Congress. I much appreciate the opportunity to come and discuss the issues we have before us. In the interest of time I'll move very quickly to a quick overview of some of the measures Canada put in place since September 11th.

Following the terrorist attacks our government quickly established an ad hoc committee of our executives on public security and anti-terrorism to address the immediate and the long term challenges. Since then the government has made significant involvement in the public safety envelope. And in our budget for 2001 shortly after September 11 there's investment of $7.7 billion over 5 years to help keep Canada safe, terrorists out and our borders open; sometimes a difficult task.

For example, There is RCMP, Royal Canadian Mounted Police which is our national police service and that was given $576 million over 5 years, for use of new technology, new members and work on national security. Our Canadian Security Intelligence Service was given $334 million for security training, approaches to new technology equipment and information systems, as well as additional personnel.

We passed an Anti-terrorism Act in 2001 to strengthen our ability to investigate, prosecute and prevent terrorist activity. We instituted a mechanism of listing of terrorists entities as identified by the U.N. Security Council and we have roughly 360 entities listed. We also listed entities under our criminal code. And once listed, an entity's assets are frozen and can be subject to seizure and forfeiture and there are penalties for dealing with them by otherwise up to 10 years in prison.

We're coordinating our law enforcement—we've heard this morning our Canadian border and ports of sea, IBITS, they're joint Canada and U.S. multi-agency enforcement teams which in this area have been working very well for cross border terrorism and criminal activities as well. Currently there are 22 teams in 11 geographic areas. And perhaps I can give you some figures on the Massena area, Congressman Souder mentioned at the Mexican border.

In 1 year period from November 2001 to December 2002 they intercepted 1,171 pounds of marijuana. Doesn't sound much compared. They intercepted $1,900 and $59,480 in U.S. currency.

42,896 cartons of cigarettes; 28 pounds of magic mushrooms; 215.5 kilograms of hashish. As well as minor smuggling decline from 2001 to 32 cases in 2002.

So our Integrated Security Enforcement Team established in Vancouver, Montreal and Ottawa, they are 200 investigative personnel who exclusively investigate terrorist threats. We have a memorandum cooperation with the United States in exchange of fingerprint records between the RCMP and the FBI. We have organization policy called Integrated Ballistics Identification Systems. Began collecting data on guns, we have a big problem with guns coming into Canada from the United States.

We have joint counter terrorism training. We just completed one in May of this year called Exercised Top Off. We're involved with the American authorities as well. We designated $600 million for border infrastructure improvements at our borders and we anticipate an announcement in the Niagara region within a few days. This initiative is to expedite the transfer of goods and services across the border, as well as security measures. Mr. Mayer will appear before you next time and he will probably have more details to share with you on that with much more authority.

We have improved security to our ports. In January of this year the government announced $172 million on new marine security programs, which is the RCMP and the Canadian police like $20 million over 5 years to increase our surveillance and tracking of marine traffic, screening of passengers and crew and the detection of criminal imports containers for radiation.

The solicit general and our national defense began a 5-year chemical biological, radiological, nuclear research and technology initiatives. There are a total currently of 41 projects ongoing and more projects are forthcoming. The RCMP instituted an Internet program, a national Web enforcement support team. We heard at great length the benefits of NEXUS and FAST. I won't go into that. On the Canadian side we have a VACIS portable unit which rotates between the Peace Bridge and Buffalo and the Lewiston Bridge. There is a second unit that has been ordered and is on its way.

The Canadian Food Inspection Agency under Agriculture Canada has been given $36.2 million over the 5-years for increased biosecurity measures at border entry ports. Increase in detection measures, increase in science laboratories and once again additional 260 member staff.

We think there's a fine cooperation in the Niagara Region between our respective agencies. Just a short example, when you went to Alert Orange there, at the request of U.S. authorities we also began—actually inspections from Canada to assist. And certainly these inspections certainly backed up the traffic going in the United States significantly and we're happy to do that for you, but we don't look forward to the next Alert Orange, that's for sure.

Louise Slaughter, your comment on the recreational boating, at any given time on a hot summer weekend there's going to be 5,000 recreational boats in Lake Erie, Basin and Niagara River and Lake Ontario Region, which is a significant problem.

Ms. SLAUGHTER. You can walk on.

Mr. MALONEY. Exactly, walking on water would be an appropriate expression. Gentlemen, I think that's just a quick overview. I'd be happy to entertain any questions you might have with myself or Mr. Lee.

Mr. SOUDER. Thank you.

We're also joined by Mr. Derek Lee, one of the Toronto writings, whose also been very active in the one initiative and many other issues on the border.

STATEMENT OF DEREK LEE, MEMBER OF PARLIAMENT, HOUSE OF COMMONS, CANADA

Mr. LEE. Thank you, Chairman Souder and Committee Chairs and members. Thank you for this opportunity. I most recently was a member of the House Special Committee on the nonmedical use of drugs. I currently also Chair the House Subcommittee on National Security. We have had a number of descriptions of the border here. I want to urge upon you a view of the border as not being the Canadian border or the U.S. border or the Mexican border, I think what we have between Canada and the United States is something rather unique, special unlike anything else in the world; both in terms of scope and complexity.

If one were to stop you as two—two-way border line, that is a Canadian two-way border and American two-way border, and view it as an organism, it is of that size and scope now that I think it's much easier to look at it that way, that border has to be managed, jointly managed to the benefit of both countries. And we in Canada certainly since September 11 come to the conclusion whether we want to be there or not with this conclusion, is that the joint management of that organism requires us to put just as much effort into making that organism work as the American's do.

While we may put different amounts of money in it, our countries are much different in size, we've got to work just as hard. And I think some of the evidence earlier today reflects all of the multilevel efforts, in fact we haven't even mentioned them all here, but that are going on daily 24 hours a day across our joint border.

The major focus of course is always the economy, the economy of both countries is heavily linked. Eighty percent of Canadian trade goes into the United States about 23 percent of American trade goes into Canada, 35 U.S. States record Canada as their best or biggest customer. That has huge implications.

I suppose I'm preaching to the converted here, this is simply a fact of life. On the drug issue, that is the main reason my colleagues have urged me to be here today and I guess why you invited me. Of course I don't speak for Canada, just as you don't speak for the United States, I'll try to explain where we've come from on the Canadian side.

The policy debate on marijuana in Canada goes back to 1970, 33 years ago when a Royal Commission on the subject urged a distinct regime be established within the whole umbrella of drug policies for marijuana and it essentially sat around for some 30 years. In May 2001, the House created the Special Committee which I sat on to deal with the nonmedical use of drugs, that's all the drugs, all illicit drugs. And in doing our work, of course, we were introduced to the utter unresolvable complexities of the drug issue, the drug problem, the drug challenge.

And we were determined to cause our government to revitalize our own Canada drug strategy. We've suggested a slightly different name, a lot more resources and some adjustments here and there. And of the 50 plus recommendations we've made, 2—only 2 dealt with marijuana. The principal one reads the committee recommends that the possession of cannabis continue to be illegal and that trafficking in any amount of cannabis remain a crime.

With that recommendation I believe the government has accepted. However, we have—we have reports of impending Canadian legislation. And that legislation, as I understand it, I haven't seen it but I understand that it will move the possession of small amounts of marijuana from the current Food and Drug Act and Criminal Code, into the Contraventions Act and marijuana convictions will be proceeded with on a ticketing type basis; procedural ticketing.

And that procedure as we understand from our research exists in 12 U.S. States. So if that were a huge problem here in the U.S.A. I'm sure the Federal Government with its very firm line and messaging, the drug issue would have moved to deal with it. And maybe the U.S. Federal Government will move to deal with it.

But at this point in time, based on the hard work of my colleagues on the Special Committee and I believe the government is there now, for many reasons that we don't have to go into today because you may end up getting it in your own countries as well. Possession of small amounts of marijuana and only that, would be prosecuted by way of the ticketing regime, if I could call it that way. I suppose if the person doesn't pay their fine they're going to go to jail but procedurally it will be done on that summary basis.

In the end, our mutual drug enforcement efforts go on. There isn't a chance in hell that the Royal Canadian Mounted Police would fail to execute on the reliable information of the source and existence of illegal drugs in Canada including marijuana. The fact, is as Congressman Souder has pointed out, we—both our countries are shipping—people in both our countries, let's put it that way, are shipping drugs across the border; it's organized crime.

And both sides of the border want to do what they can to squeeze it, to pinch it and to eradicate it. That's what Americans call the War On Drugs, that's what the Canadians call the National Drug Strategy. We're both moving in the same direction I hope. And I hope that the press reports of legalization won't be taken too seriously. We intend to increase penalties, as I understand it, for certain types of trafficking and the marijuana growers, which are hydroponic. I believe we're going to create a new offense. So let's see what happens, that legislation should be added into the House soon.

The most important part of why I really wanted to be here today was to participate in an exercise that reflects the sharing of information across the border. Fairly certain that 80 to 90 percent of all the issues and problems our two countries deal with, from time to time, are manageable, simply by talking and listening and sharing in the evolution of the solution.

So I'm delighted to have a chance to be a part of this exercise and I congratulate your House for allowing this to happen. And I hope that our House can do the same on an as needed basis, from time to time. Thank you.

Mr. SOUDER. Before I give the mic back to Chairman Camp, I want to just say that I think that this is very important as you deal with homeland security or subcommittees to involve both the representatives of Canada and Mexico in particular in the discussions, because it is so important in our trade and commerce and immigration questions clearly while we talk about illegal immigrants. The United States could not operate and we'd have to figure out how to get a reasonable water strategy that still protects us from illegal narcotics and terrorism.

I also want to say for the record that I don't agree with Mr. Lee's description of their proposal. But I felt it was important that we had on the record here what their position is because this is gonna be one of the most hotly debated things if this goes through on the border, parliamentary discussions it was clear that the Canadians even in the different parties are arguing among themselves. It's not clear that this legislation is gonna move forth and maybe introduce, not move through.

We've talked about technical changes, we've been debating on CBC, TV, radio, but it is a process for us to work through. Their committee, in the House and the Senate both came down to our Congress to meet with the different leaders. And if we're going to effectively work as both a North American zone with our neighboring nations, we have to be very particular in the Homeland Security Border Subgroup of how to work these things through.

And what I found a lot of times is when the different groups come to Washington, nobody really wants to meet with them as much. And today's interest in this hearing is really important because having a number of members who are willing to do this on a regular basis, is going to make it a lot more effective. Because if we can get harmonization and understand each other at the border, we don't cripple the commerce. I have had more than my share of time to cross discuss with both of these gentlemen and both of them are big advocates of trade and in trying to work together and I appreciate the leadership.

Mr. CAMP. Thank you. Thank you both for testifying and for being here and taking the time out of your every day to do that. I would just associate myself with Chairman Souder's remarks on the issue. I think when we look at harmonization, I think it does have implications for how we work together to protect this border. And there's been some very good projects, I think the reverse inspections, customs inspections, obviously the Smart Border Initiative and I think it's really the direction that everyone needs to be going.

I would just say in my State of Michigan, I don't know if we're on your list of 12 States but really it's cities, there are cities in the United States that have done that. And so I would just be cautious of that, that there are some city jurisdictions that have made that distinction, maybe not the entire State.

Just tell me how you think the—I guess I'll start with Mr. Maloney, how you think this sort of joint management of the border is going and what do you think we can do to make it work better?

Mr. MALONEY. I think it's going very well. We talked a little bit here early this morning about the possibility of an international zone. I think the integration of our respective agencies would certainly work much better if that was established, with U.S. personnel being able to work in Canada and perhaps vice versa, even at the administrative level, as far as the operations.

Currently the toll collectors on the American side, we have much more room on the Canadian side, which if they were brought to Canada it would free up more land which would double the truck capacity on the American side going into the United States. And these are the type of—just increasing and augmenting the joint interactions going on now is the most important. The IBIT program is an ideal example on how it can work.

Mr. CAMP. Mr. Lee, your comments on that?

Mr. LEE. I think to be successful with these two countries we've got to look—although there is certainly immediate concerns, real existing threats that have to be dealt with, we've got to deal with those. But to be successful in the long run, I think we've to try to get outside the box a little bit and look down the road 5 or 10 years or even longer, because whatever is there now is going to get bigger.

The infrastructure, it's not going to shrink. It's just going to get bigger. And Congressman Souder told a story about the experiment in Sweet Grass Montana and they're building a one unit to deal with the border. It sounds pretty good until they had to design in the washrooms and they realized that if they put the washrooms on the Canadian side of the border, then the American's who were carrying firearms wouldn't be able to wash without leaving their guns behind, simply because Canada had a regime of firearm control.

So it sounds silly but it's an example of how the administration when they go up to do this work, half the work is on the law on the regulations that exist. They're not permitted to go outside the box. So who is going to think outside box to get us there? Well, it's partly the legislators and the policymakers. And that's a conceptual answer but there are smart people on both sides of the border and pretty good resources and I know we're going to revolve in the right direction. In fact, I think this organism of the border is so big it's bigger than all of us and it's going to drag us along into the future one way or the other.

Mr. CAMP. Tell me what you think about the automated entry and exiting system that have been proposed, what are your thoughts of that?

Mr. MALONEY. The difficulty as I see it is the traffic density. It's just gonna not only clog the border, it will strangle the border. That's the difference that we've got. Certainly we have the need to have—know where people are going and perhaps where they're coming, but just the reliability of it, it certainly won't wash.

The NEXUS program is where you've been preapproved, low risk people, they go through the criminality checks, security checks on both sides of the border, that is certainly the way we should be going. But I have real difficulties with the automated system, just the time alone it's going to be tough.

Mr. CAMP. OK. Any comment on that?

Mr. LEE. Just that any pinch point that malfunctions or even a badly placed stop sign or the system breaks like involving a broken water main in Windsor, Ontario, any infrastructure pinch point is going to have economic implications. So it needs constant thought, reworking and that's going on now. But it's just going to take a lot of work to get it right and think how we do things now.

Mr. CAMP. Thank you.

Ms. SANCHEZ. Thank you, Mr. Chairman. I've just kind of been chuckling over here when I hear about your fears of commerce being slighted because of long waits at the border. You should come and see our borders at California, New Mexico.

Mr. SOUDER. Could you give an idea of the waits in California and what they're looking at here?

Ms. SANCHEZ. As I said, Saturday night I was crossing, Sunday night—Saturday, I can't remember, this is any time. It used to be you could call ahead or if you had plans, they could go check the border for you and tell when you could cross within 20 minutes. Currently, at any given time the wait is at least an hour and a half. When I crossed over on Saturday it was 2½ hours, that's without the pre-checking out and everything. If you're in the special line to cross, it usually will take you about half an hour to 40 minutes, so we have a lot of commerce that goes across.

You might have two or three booths open, we have 24 open across San Isidro and you're talking about an hour and a half, 2½, 3 hour waits. And this has been going on for a while. So what would be the times that you all are looking at right now and what's your fear?

Mr. LEE. I think the broken water main was what, 6 hours?

Ms. SLAUGHTER. 7½.

Mr. LEE. 7½ hour delay, but that was a 1-day wonder. It was a bad day. We couldn't carry on. All of these huge businesses, what do we do $1.2 , $1.4 billion across the border every day.

Ms. SANCHEZ. We do more on the southern border by the way, that's nothing. That's nothing. I'll get you the number but it's nothing, that's like a drop in the bucket.

Mr. LEE. I'm going to beg to differ. I am told that the $1.2, $1.4 billion a day is the largest trade relationship in the world. It doesn't exist anywhere else. Not to underestimate your favorite border crossing the U.S.-Mexico.

Ms. SANCHEZ. It's not my favorite anymore by the way.

Mr. SOUDER. There's more total sales product value in the north, more trucks in the south and far more people in the south. And so both borders—but the important thing to note from our perspective because what she's describing in California, is also true with the Texas crossings. When you all raised the infrastructure questions and then we raised—look, I'm on the north side. But the fact is that they're yelling at the south border for more lanes because the length of time every day and in the middle of the night is longer.

Mr. MALONEY. Mr. Chairman, we have delays of that length as well; 2, 2½ hours. They're put on the radio for truck traffic, what the wait is at the Lewiston Bridge, what the wait is at the Peace

Bridge. The inter traffic is somewhat laxed generally but sometimes you get caught in the line up of trucks with the infrastructure and you're caught there as well. The length of time in delivery is a real key item here, we have here the Tonawanda Plant, places where motor vehicles have to be in Toronto the next day.

Horticulture is a big industry here in the Niagara peninsula. Flowers are picked and put into transport freight and sent to New York City. If there's a significant delay at the border that impairs their product. Also we're concerned about your border as well because a lot of your product comes up to us too. So it's not as if we're in isolation. We have the same problems as you. Our infrastructure is not quite as large as yours having that many booths but we still have the same problems.

Ms. SANCHEZ. Yes. That was a quote for just a regular type of tourist type of crossing the border. Trucks are an even bigger problem, the commerce that goes across, we're all concerned about the commerce that's why I bring it up. Let me just—I have really have no questions other than to say that I believe and I don't really know this because I don't do drugs, so I don't really check the State law quite frankly, but I do believe that California is one of those places that allows an ounce or less of personal possession and you get the equivalent of a misdemeanor or ticket written, to which you have to pay a fine and go to court or what have you, or actually I think send in your money and it doesn't matter. So that's the law of the land in California, I believe.

And we also of course have passed by popular initiative medicinal marijuana which at the State level we are more happy than not to have that in place. The Federal Government is a different situation and continues to test the waters and shut down what we have with respect to medicinal marijuana. But you're probably talking to the only member here who represents a constituency that's way far ahead on this whole issue.

And I'll just end by saying my district is a very Republican and Libertarian district, the area that I represent. And I almost lost one time to a Republican who his whole platform was to advocate that we make drugs legal basically, so California is significantly ahead on the whole marijuana issue at least. Thank you.

Mr. SOUDER. Mr. Sweeney.

Mr. SWEENEY. Thank you, Mr. Chairman.

Mr. Maloney, welcome, thank you very much for your testimony. I found it of great importance and great interest. As you probably heard earlier in the testimony, I'm from the eastern end of this State and have a lot of concern and interest in the development of the Champlain border crossing. I will note that of the top 10 lane crossings in this nation, 3 of those top 10 are in this sector; from Champlain down to Alexandria Bay to the Niagara frontier. Also, I was able to a year ago secure $2 million in study money that we're working with your colleagues from Ontario in developing the New York to Montreal corridor and how we could make that more efficient.

So the Champlain border and the border crossing issues have been issues for years that we've been concerned with. I'd be interested in hearing some general comments from you on the distinctions between the challenges over at Champlain versus what we face here on the Niagara side. And in particular, do it to make the point that the NEXUS system which is something I think is gonna be of great benefit toward further enhancing the relationship of that living organism that is the border on the list of Champlain and has been for some time. What's your thoughts on that notion and idea and how important that border crossing is as well.

Mr. MALONEY. Currently the NEXUS program and even the FAST program, it hasn't been going as quickly as we anticipated but it is coming. There has been natural reasons, people have been reluctant to cross our borders. As I understand it the facts that I'm aware of approximately 15,000 applied in the FAST program, 5,000 under the NEXUS program. But I can see this is the system or the solution all the way along our border, from the maritime zone to the west coast. I think that's the way to go.

You know, I spoke with a young woman in the grocery store 2 weeks ago and she had applied for a NEXUS card at the end of February and still hadn't been called in for an interview so there are logistical problems——

Mr. SWEENEY. Safe to say we need to expedite all those systems?

Mr. MALONEY. Well, I think we're doing that. In this area all the inspections have been done on the American side and now they're starting to come to the Canadian side as well.

Mr. SWEENEY. Sure. Mr. Lee.

Mr. LEE. I'm very confident that where the two countries are working on the particular project together, there will be success. And some of the factors are the political support for that and I'm very pleased to hear of your support and new investments in that. But whether the political push for it advances this concept or advances in time, in other words, hurry up political push, both will help with those projects. The getting out in front, getting outside the box. Pushing the administration to advance in concepts so that it will serve the needs for the years to come.

And to be bold in doing that. Because there seems to be a lot of—the resistance on both sides of the border at one time based on sense of sovereignty, sense of ownership of the border, this is our border; that has receded. Even though you think it might go up because of marijuana on our side of the border, Canadian's side of the border, Canadians have a lot more tolerance for the joint management concept. They would not be as sensitive to an American role in managing their border. They see it now as something we've got to do together.

Mr. SWEENEY. Mr. Lee, I couldn't agree more. I think we're in an interesting time ironically. On one end we need the security required, different commitments and attention, and then the recognition that in terms of the economy. And frankly, in an effort to not let the terrorists win the fight, we need to continue to go forward in those areas.

Let me—I was going to get to some specific question, you in particular as chairman of the Intelligence Committee in Parliament could answer. Let me just ask you a very broad question about what changes occurred in Canada, subsequent to the attacks of September 11th, in intelligence gathering and in terms of the priorities that you had to establish in order to meet a burgeoning threat that wasn't just the main land the United States but the entire continent. And maybe you can give me some sense of the mood at Parliament and the commitment or not of your colleagues.

Mr. LEE. On a general level, the whole House of Commons and Senate pretty much across the board bought into the challenge which seemed to be an American challenge. September 11 was an American event but there were many other people around the world involved, many other victims. So Canadians had no doubt that they were going to be involved in whatever evolved out of September 11.

As you know, all of your intelligence services had all the infrastructure pre-September 11. It was all out there. Maybe it wasn't as tight as it could have been, maybe there were visions that should have happened earlier that weren't. But without trying to figure out exactly what happened, post September 11, there has been a significant tightening up in Canada and additional resources—the counter terrorism Branch Sesus will have more weight, more resources, more infrastructure added into it and we've made multi-million dollar investments. Mr. Maloney has described it briefly.

So we have resourced significantly, both Sesus and the Royal Canadian Mounted Police to deal with the counter terrorist initiative. Even though we don't feel Canada is a target, we could be in Canada. But we feel like we're part of the program with our American neighbors, we have no choice but to be very involved in that.

Mr. SWEENEY. If I could just interrupt. Is that because you haven't felt as though there has been a direct attack on the persons of Canada and the property of Canada, or is that based on some other valuation?

Mr. LEE. Do we see the terrorist threat out there on Canadian soil, yes, we gather intelligence and we'd like to think we're on top of the potential threats. But I don't think in Canada we've ever experienced anything as ugly and conspiratorial as the Al-Queda threat. This is outside the envelope. So now we're reconstructing, as you are in the U.S.A. To deal with this ugly conspiratorial threat that's come right to your homeland.

I mean, it came right here, we can't be isolated from that. We trade data with your guys, if we can put it that way and with other intelligence agencies around the world ensuring that and dog everything to ensure that.

Mr. MALONEY. I mentioned the Anti-terrorism Act and shortly after the incident and there are a lot of people who were concerned about civil rights, charter rights, very concerned about the new restrictions and investigative power. Fortunately as time passes, we see these have not been abused, but even the suggestion initially that some of those terrorists might have come from Canada, that was a very sensitive issue in Canada. We were glad that the 19 in fact did not come from Canada, and we're very aware of that as well. The Phantom Five that we're also alleged to becoming to do dirty deeds in the United States from Canada, they didn't exist.

We're very sensitive to those. And we feel that we're just as much a North American continent, we're as vulnerable as you are. We certainly have supported you in Afghanistan, and we could be targets too. Eighty-five percent of our trade goes across these bridges, in Detroit, the Niagara area. If you knock those out, it will knock our economy out. But we're in this together for the long haul and I think that's the way most Canadians feel.

Mr. SWEENEY. While the linkages are real, as a New Yorker and a Member, I thank you for your testimony and I hope and believe that we will continue to work as cooperative as we can.

Mr. SOUDER. Because we're in a deep time bind on what we've worked out here, as Congressman Shadegg has one more question, Congresswoman Slaughter has a brief comment, Congresswoman Jackson Lee has agreed to yield her time to be the first questioner on the next panel, because we want to make sure before many of the Members have to leave that we can hear the testimony. Mr. Shadegg.

Mr. SHADEGG. Mr. Chairman, I'll try to work this into a single statement and question and just request that you look into this issue and perhaps get back to us, it may be of help and assistance. Canada like America is an open and free society. You have an interest in acquiring immigrant workers. I have been provided some information that says that 95 percent of foreigners claiming refugee status are immediately allowed to settle in Canada even though upwards of half of them have no identification.

The statistics I've been given suggest that Canada accepted 15,000 refugees since September 11th, this is from Joe Bassett. Of those 15,000, some 2,500 came from terrorist countries; Algeria, Pakistan and Afghanistan. I also understand according to this information that Deputy Prime Minister John Manley says Canada's current domestic security priority or current domestic security policy is under review. Are you aware of that view and are you watching it and working with—that once into Canada, access in the United States is much greater and probably vice versa? Are you A, aware of the review and B, looking at it in a cooperative sense with the United States? And if you don't want to answer that at this point, we'd be happy to take an answer——

Mr. LEE. I'm a politician, I'm happy to answer your question. The answer is, yes, we're working on this and including the particulars you mentioned. I was asked by an American media program a half a year or year ago, about all these refugees that Canada has that aren't documented. My reply was you know where half our refugees come from, do you know Congressman?

Mr. SHADEGG. I don't know that I do.

Mr. LEE. The United States. So, I mean, to complain that all of these refugees in Canada are undocumented when they're coming across the border from United States to Canada, please try to understand where they enter. And in addition to that, we have signed an agreement, a Safe Third-Country Agreement with the U.S.A. And we are waiting in the utmost good faith for the United States to develop some regulations and we're hoping they'll be there. The Safe Third-Country Agreement will actually allow those good refugees in the United States to be processed in the United States as opposed to Canada, then you won't have to worry about them.

But your point is well taken. Our efforts to better document and assure the integrity in terms of a terrorist threat of everybody who's coming into Canada, including those post abroad, interdict abroad. In jointly with the Americans we do this. That's in process and we're getting better at it everyday.

Mr. SHADEGG. I appreciate that very much.

Mr. MALONEY. Actually, the Niagara region is the largest land border crossing for refugees coming into Canada, coming obviously from the United States, coming up from Central America or from New York and up through Buffalo. We're certainly looking at that again and more resources, again off-shore applications and a prompter review of refugee applications is the way you should go.

It's also a concern as we've seen with the SARS situation. We have a proposal in Fort Erie where it's a one stop shop, when they come across they have their interviews done, have their physicals done. So if tuberculosis, they know it right away, whether we have a problem health wise with these people coming into the country too which is another area of security, health security.

Mr. SHADEGG. Thank you very much.

Mr. SOUDER. Congresswoman Jackson Lee from Immigration prompted an additional question from her because this is her major area of focus.

Ms. JACKSON LEE. The Congressman from Arizona just probed an area and I will be brief and I have acknowledged to the chairman that I will lose my front position on the next panel. But it's so urgent that I wanted to make sure I asked.

It's an interesting question that most of the refugees come from the United States. Can you tell me whether or not you've changed requirements for the admission of individuals from the Caribbean to Canada since September 11 and why and—how can we since we have this mutual challenge with respect to refugees and also the undocumented, how can we collaborate; United States and Americans on ensuring that one, we balance the theory that I've utilized that immigration does not equate to terrorism and that both foundations I think have benefited from immigrants but yet we have a new responsibility since September 11?

Mr. LEE. We have a new Immigration Act in force in Canada but that would not materially impact on the immigration coming from the Caribbean.

Ms. JACKSON LEE. You ask them for different documentation?

Mr. LEE. You might be referring to is—well, all of our immigrants are screened, all of our legal immigration is screened and security cleared and this is not the problem area. It's the visitors, the visitors that come without visas.

What has happened since September 11 is that we kind of regretted that we had to do it, but we've now imposed a cross Caribbean visa requirement; to come from the Caribbean you've got to get a visa. And before that there was some Caribbean countries, like I think it's Grenada, where you didn't need a visa to make a visit to Canada; it was being abused a little bit here and there—not just by Grenadians.

So, we have paper secured the movement of the visitors from the Caribbean to Canada now and that's working its way through the system.

Ms. JACKSON LEE. And is there any ways of collaboration—so that's only for the non-immigrant visitor that's coming in that's not coming to stay, but they're visiting?

Mr. LEE. Well, in order to get to Canada from the Caribbean you got to fly—or you don't have to, you could take a long boat. But now we are now sharing our passenger—airline passenger lists. And the extent to which we share, I'm not an expert on, but it's caused some concern for Canadians, the extent to which airline passengers lists are now being shared. But we've had to do it to fly planes around North America. So there is one vehicle to deal with security issues if the need arises and it's probably happening now.

Ms. JACKSON LEE. On the Caribbean—and this is my last question—on the Caribbean did you hold hearings or what was the basis of changing your policy?

Mr. LEE. Unfortunately it just happened very quickly. I believe it was a collaboration between Canada and United States and both countries, whereas Canada felt that it simply had no choice but to impose the visa requirement. And politically I represent eighty percent immigrant, it's a huge percentage and I've taken some heat for that, administered the imposition of the visa requirement. It was not done with huge consultation. But our diplomats, our immigration people were aware of this. The problem that we were encountering, the risks that were there, and I believe we felt that was the only solution to reduce the risk in the light of September 11 and the airline industry risks.

Ms. JACKSON LEE. Thank you. Thank you, Mr. Chairman.

Mr. SOUDER. Thank you. I appreciate your testimony and the work of both of you. The third panel could come forward so we can get you sworn in and started.

[Witnesses sworn.]

Mr. SOUDER. Let the record show all witnesses respond in the affirmative. I think what we'll do is start with Mr. Beilein.

STATEMENT OF THOMAS A. BEILEIN, SHERIFF, NIAGARA COUNTY SHERIFF'S DEPARTMENT

Mr. BEILEIN. Chairman Souder, Chairman Camp, distinguished members of the subcommittee. I am Thomas Beilein, the sheriff of the county of Niagara, NY. I am a law enforcement professional with 34 years of experience responsible for keeping the peace and protecting the citizens of Niagara County. It is certainly my honor to be asked to testify here today and I thank you for your privilege.

What is unique about Niagara County is that we share an international border with Canada; to our west and to our north. From the cataracts above Niagara Falls to our eastern border with Orleans County, there are approximately 40 miles of international border. There are three international points of entry into Niagara County; two of them are in the city of Niagara Falls and one is in the Town of Lewiston.

In the year 2002, approximately 4½ million vehicles crossed from Canada to the United States using these points of entry. It is common knowledge there are no jurisdictional constraints on crime and criminals. Because our unique location and because of the amount of traffic that flows to and from Canada, law enforcement has always maintained a good working relationship with both our Federal agencies and our law enforcement counterparts in Canada.

This relationship includes drug investigations, criminal investigations, intelligence sharing, along with search and rescue recovery operations in the Niagara River and Lake Ontario. President

Kennedy once said, "Geography has made us neighbors, history has made us friends, economics has made us partners and necessity has made us allies."

Local law enforcement has an outstanding list of accomplishments when working in unison with Canadian law enforcement. We also can point to a similar list of accomplishments when working with our own Federal agencies. Although communication with our Canadian counterparts is an ongoing process, on several occasions we have taken our relationship to a higher level. I would like to document a couple of those occasions.

On the Green Ribbon Task Force between May 1987 and December 1992, this multi-jurisdictional Task Force was responsible for the investigation and prosecution in Canada of Paul Bernardo and Tammy Homolka, serial rapists, who were convicted of sexually assaulting 18 women and killing 3 others. Paul Bernardo had visited Niagara County several times during that period. Working with Canadian authorities we tracked his whereabouts when he was here, we assisted in providing documentation of those visits and determined that he had not committed a crime in the United States.

Operation Ovech, during the later half of 1997 and 1998 we had investigators from the Royal Canadian Mounted Police, Niagara Regional Police, London Police Services, Ontario Provincial Police, Customs Canada, United States Customs, United States Drug Enforcement Administration, along with our Sheriff's Office, conducted an investigation into cross-border trafficking in Ecstasy.

In July 1998, this investigation culminated with the arrest of 12 individuals for violation of the Controlled Drugs and Substance Act in Canada and two individuals in the United States. During this investigation 29 ounces of cocaine were purchased, weapons were seized, along with vehicles and assortment of stolen property.

Working together with our own Federal agencies has been a positive experience. I have officers currently assigned with the Joint Terrorism Task Force in Buffalo, the Drug Enforcement Regional Task Force, the Bureau of Alcohol and Firearms Regional Task Force, both of those agencies also have quarters in Buffalo, NY. All three of these Task Forces can list major accomplishments.

Three of these accomplishments, you mentioned three, would be the Al-Queda Sleeper Cell located in Lackawanna, NY; where six members of the Lackawanna Community were arrested for attending terrorists camps in Afghanistan. I believe as of this morning's news all six had agreed to plead guilty to some charges.

The investigation into a laborers local organization crime investigation conducted with the FBI and U.S. Attorney's Office, along with the Niagara Falls Police Department. A major investigation with the Drug Enforcement Administration, Operation Deja Vu, which was an investigation which investigated the illegal importation of cocaine starting in Colombia and ending in western New York and southern Ontario.

It is necessary to emphasize to this committee that every successful joint investigation needs three key ingredients. We need a pool of skillful, experienced and dedicated officers. We also need highly skilled leadership capable of managing those investigations. And third, the financial resources that only the Federal Government can provide.

Despite the successes and effectiveness of these Task Forces and despite cooperation with Canadian and U.S. law enforcement, there still exists major concerns regarding the security of our border. There are numerous inlets and coves along the southern shore of Lake Ontario that have a history of being popular with smugglers. Inlets that sport such names as Keg Creek, earned those names during the prohibition when alcohol was commonly smuggled into the country. The fact is that from the Toronto Harbor in downtown Toronto to any number of inlets and harbors in Niagara County, it is only a 30 minute boat ride. A ride across the vast waterway that is only sporadically patrolled. From the Queenston Ontario docks just north of the Lewiston-Queenston Bridge the Lewiston sand docks is a short paddle in a rubber raft.

Within the past 3 months this vulnerability of this area has been documented by two incidents. A 7-year-old Canadian boy rode his bike to the Whirlpool Bridge, threw his sister's bike over the bridge and into the gorge and walked into the United States unconfronted. Local law enforcement questioned him when he appeared not to belong in the area and determined that he had left his home in Niagara Falls, Ontario for an afternoon adventure.

On March 31st, six people who tried to enter the United States after crossing the Niagara River were apprehended while calling a cab. They actually landed approximately 1:30 a.m., and weren't detected until 3 a.m., while walking down Main Street in Lewiston, NY. All six were determined to be illegal aliens who entered across the Niagara River.

Both of these cases demonstrate how vulnerable our border security in Niagara County is. It also shows the difficulty in securing our borders and protecting our citizens. We need to prevent terrorists from entering through a border that can be entered by a determined 7 year-old. Local law enforcement is ready and willing to assist in those efforts, however, we need your help in gaining additional resources in order to accomplish this.

Mr. Chairman, I applaud this committee for the work you have donein addressing the issues facing our borders. Not withstanding this past week's terrorists events, a recent United Nations report indicated a drastic decrease in terrorist incidents in this past year. This reflects your dedication and the ongoing efforts that face us. Working together I feel we can ensure the security of those who we are sworn to protect. Thank you.

Mr. SOUDER. Thank you very much.

Mr. Deveso, is that correct? Deveso, I apologize, thank you very much for your testimony.

STATEMENT OF RUSSELL DEVESO, CHAIRMAN, NYS MOTOR TRUCK ASSOCIATION, INC., GENERAL MANAGER, G.W. BURNETT, INC., BUFFALO, NY

Mr. DEVESO. Thank you. The New York State Motor Truck Association is the voice of the trucking industry in New York State. On behalf of the Motor Truck membership and the industry, I would like to thank Chairman Camp, Chairman Souder and the congressional committee for the opportunity to speak on the issue of improving security and facilitating commerce at the northern border.

Every State has a State trucking association affiliated with the American Trucking Associations [ATA]. At the State level, members are encouraged to join and follow association-endorsed programs. By reaching out to nonmembers, membership growth is promoted and so are the programs and educational opportunities. Throughout the year, we keep the entire industry informed of changes, not only in the regulatory arena but also in safety, maintenance, technology and operations. We accomplish this through mass mailings, Web site news, blast fax, seminars and outreach programs.

The Federal Motor Carrier Safety Administration regulates and the Motor Truck Industry implements areas of employment screening which is a vital part of the process of recruiting and hiring new truck drivers. The industry utilizes automated services that provide a full range of employment screening of motor vehicle reports, criminal history checks, consumer credit reports, commercial drivers licenses, a drug and alcohol screening and hazardous material hauling certification.

But the industry does not simply comply with regulations. In the War on Terrorism it has voluntarily stepped forward to assist in this worthwhile and vital effort. Three million truck drivers eyes will act as the eyes and ears for our nation. Under the "Highway Watch Program," professional truck drivers are trained to spot and report any suspicious activity that might have terrorism or national security implications. Their goal, to make certain a truck is never used as a weapon.

The FAST Program—Free and Secure Trade—is a bilateral initiative between United States and Canada, designed to ensure security and safety while enhancing the economic prosperity of both countries. The New York State Motor Truck Association is happy to offer any expertise or insight we have to assure that FAST exceeds expectations.

When all processes are implemented, the missing puzzle piece is the vital and overwhelming call for improvements to perfected infrastructure. This must include dedicated and adequate truck lanes and booths, increased customs and inspection personnel, and enough room to handle future volumes of commercial traffic. Even a small child would have to pass through a guarded turnstile.

The mission of the New York State Motor Truck Association is to serve and represent the interests of the trucking industry; to enhance the industry's image; efficiency, productivity and competitiveness; promote highway safety, provide educational programs and work for a healthy business environment. And we thank you for this opportunity.

Mr. SOUDER. Thank you very much.

We'll now hear from Mr. Kevin Feely, the Chapter Director of the National Treasury Employees Union.

STATEMENT OF KEVIN FEELY, PRESIDENT, CHAPTER 154, NATIONAL TREASURY EMPLOYEES UNION

Mr. FEELY. Thank you. Chairman Souder, Chairman Camp, Ranking Member Sanchez, distinguished committee members, thank you for the opportunity to provide testimony about northern border security and the Port of Buffalo/Niagara Falls, NY. I am proud to be one of the over 12,000 Customs employees who along with Immigration and Naturalization Service, Border Patrol, and APHIS inspectors were merged to form the Bureau of Customs and Border Protection, within the Border and Transportation Security Directorate of the Department of Homeland Security on March 1, 2003.

Customs personnel make up the first line of defense against terrorism, illegal immigration and the influx of drugs and contraband at 317 ports of entry across the United States. The scope of the task is enormous. Nationwide in fiscal year 2002 nearly 415 million travelers, including 118 million cars and trucks and over $1 trillion worth of commercial merchandise were processed entering the United States. This number continues to grow annually and statistics show that over the last decade, trade has increased by 135 percent.

During my 29 years as a Customs Inspector I have personally witnessed the exponential growth of border traffic. When I first started there was only one truck lane at the Peace Bridge with no waiting. Now, there are four lanes and trucks often line the entire span of the bridge even backing up on to the highway approaches. In 1976 when I was first assigned here to the Rainbow Bridge in Niagara Falls, in the dead of winter you could hear the water rushing over the falls because that was the only activity around. Scenic tourism was the only attraction.

Now there are casinos on both sides of the border. In terms of traffic, in fiscal year 2002, four bridges entering the United States in the Port of Buffalo/Niagara Falls, more than 7 million passenger vehicles and over 1 million commercial trucks were processed. The United States has 5,525 miles of border with Canada, nearly three times as long as the U.S. border with Mexico.

As the traffic has increased, I watched the staffing in my port first decrease and then stagnate as it did across all of the northern border. Increased resources were concentrated on the southern border where the threat was perceived to be higher. Then just prior to the Millennium Celebration, Customs Inspector Diana Dean in Port Angeles, WA thwarted a terrorist attack planned for New Years Day 2000 at the Los Angeles International Airport.

For the first time, security at the northern border was tightened and many inspectors were temporarily transferred from other parts of the country since the staffing numbers along the northern border were inadequate. Once the Millennium Celebrations had passed with no actual terrorist attacks having occurred our staffing levels returned to normal.

Then, on September 11, 2001, our complacency was shattered. Since then, more attention has finally been focused on the northern border and it is my hope that Congress will continue to increase funding for personnel and resources at my port, as well as not only our northern border ports, but all ports of entry. In addition to annual appropriations, Customs also receives funds from a user fee account known as the COBRA account. This user fee account funds all inspector's and canine enforcement officers' overtime pay, as well as approximately 1,200 Customs positions across the country. The COBRA account is funded with user fees collected from air and sea passengers, commercial vehicles, commercial vessels and rail cars entering the United States.

The COBRA fund will expire on September 30, 2003, unless it is reauthorized by Congress before then. Currently, there is provision incentive bill No. 1054, Jobs and Growth Tax Relief Reconciliation Act of 2003 that reauthorizes COBRA until September 30, 2013. However, there is no COBRA reauthorization provision in the House passed tax bill. The COBRA fund must be reauthorized or Congress must appropriate additional funds to make up for the loss of the user fees.

As a representative of the front line Customs employees of the National Treasury Employees Union, Chapter 154, I have serious concerns regarding our transition into the Department of Homeland Security. As a result of the Homeland Security Act of 2002, the administration was given new Federal personnel flexibilities in a number of areas governing the current rights of Federal employees. While it was unclear exactly what is meant by flexibilities, the members I represent fear that the flexibilities that will likely be proposed by the administration will lead to many fewer dedicated personnel being willing to work for the new department. That would be a shame and I hope Congress will not let that happen.

I'd ask the members of this committee to use the oversight authority given to you to ensure that Title 5 rights and benefits that currently available to the employees who have been merged into this new department are not lost. In addition, for 27 years as an officer of NTEU I have lobbied Congress in an attempt to gain law enforcement officer status for Customs Inspectors and Canine Enforcement Officers. We must carry a weapon and at least three times a year qualify and maintain proficiency on a firearm range. We also have the authority to arrest and detain those engaged in smuggling drugs and violating other civil and criminal laws. In addition, nationwide fiscal year 2002, Customs personnel seized more than 165 pounds of cocaine, 1.2 million pounds of marijuana and over 4,000 pounds of heroin.

Unfortunately, we are still not considered law enforcement officers like our Customs and Border Protection counterparts in the Border Patrol. We have long performed law enforcement duties and we deserve the recognition and benefits that come with law enforcement officer status. We face real dangers on a daily basis and granting us law enforcement officer status would be an appropriate and long overdue step in recognizing and retaining the Customs and Border Protection personnel who continue to protect our borders from terrorism, drugs, contraband and illegal immigration.

I understand the House Government Reform Committee will be holding a hearing on this issue in the near future. I hope that you will attend that hearing and support law enforcement officer status for Customs officers. I also hope the members of this committee will go back to Washington and tell your colleagues and the administration, what you have seen here and how important additional funding is for Customs and Border Protection personnel in New York and around the country.

In closing, thank you for the opportunity to comment on these very important issues, as I submit this testimony on behalf of all my colleagues in the Bureau of Customs and Border Protection, especially the employees here at the Port of Buffalo/Niagara Falls, NY.

Mr. SOUDER. Thank you very much.

Ms. Hamilton.

STATEMENT OF DAWN HAMILTON, DIRECTOR OF STRATEGIC PLANNING, WNED

Ms. HAMILTON. Chairman Souder, Chairman Camp and Distinguished Members of Congress, thank you for the opportunity to testify today. I'm Dawn Hamilton, Director of Strategic Planning for WNED, Western New York Public Broadcasting Association. It is clear one of the greater challenges in our homeland security is to improve the speed, the flexibility and coordination of information sharing among local, State agencies, Federal Government and first responders.

Public television will soon offer a wireless broadband distribution and networking solution that can transmit information instantaneously to one individual or an unlimited number of agencies and responders. For all public television stations, digital broadcasting is mandated by the FCC. And as of Saturday night, WNED is transmitting a digital signal.

With digital television we can transmit data as information. We can bring pictures, sound, text and graphics into bits of information using a digital signal and it can be transmitted securely and instantaneously. Here's an example of how it could work. A Federal agency needs to communicate information immediately about a biohazard. That information is transmitted by a satellite to a secure server at WNED. The information is encrypted and transmitted as data through digital broadcasting. But only people with PCs and laptops with a special TV tuner card programmed to receive and encrypt this information will actually receive the data. The same distribution system can work for local law agencies as well. And the software has been developed so that it would automatically activate the data access system without any direct action or intervention by WNED.

The organization which is distributing the information, whether it be Federal, State or local agencies, would have complete control over who receives what information and when. Most emergency responders and government agencies involved in disaster preparedness already have PCs and laptops. All that would be needed would be a tuner card that looks like this, the cost is $300, and an antenna; a silver sensor that looks like this which costs about $30 at Radio Shack. Unfortunately, they were sold out in the Buffalo area this weekend.

If you have a roof top antenna, that would serve the same purpose. Public television is only a distribution mechanism. We would have no knowledge, no control or access to any sensitive data that might be transmitted. The border is also not a barrier for digital broadcasting. WNED's digital signal now serves most of Western New York; the entire Niagara peninsula of Ontario and well beyond the Toronto Metropolitan area.

We can transmit vital information to agencies and first responders on both sides of the border easily and seamlessly. Next. If there was a bio-hazard situation in our region it would be very important to get projections about contamination fallouts to first responders. The scenario that's depicted here shows a wind shift about 1 hour after contamination that clearly impacts the best evacuation routes outside of a contamination area.

This will be vital information for law enforcement officials to act as quickly as possible. Firefighters on the scene would like information details, the procedures to effectively respond with bio-hazards, bxlueprints for buildings. And local hospitals could be sent information on treatment for incoming casualties and appropriate decontamination procedures. Regional broadcasting can communicate this information and much more, instantly and effectively.

In conclusion, WNED in the Buffalo/Niagara region and public broadcasting across the continent can provide for the timely transmission, security, congestion free access, addressibility and scaleability that is cost effective. Public broadcasting, we consider ourselves the community connection. And we would welcome the opportunity to help you connect with the great people who protect, who respond, who treat and who lead the way in times of crisis. Thank you for your kind attention and your thoughtful consideration, and I'd be glad to answer any questions you may have.

Mr. SOUDER. Thank you. I understand that you've got a back pain, if you want to go back over and sit in the other——

Ms. HAMILTON. Thank you.

Mr. SOUDER. Mr. Mayer.

STATEMENT OF STEPHEN MAYER, GENERAL MANAGER/OPERATIONS, BUFFALO & FORT ERIE PUBLIC BRIDGE AUTHORITY

Mr. MAYER. Chairman Souder and Chairman Camp, thank you very much, and members of the committee.

I'm going to speak to you today as a crossing operator and if it's OK with you, I will not go through my testimony, you have it in the record. So I would like to just focus on some of the highlights and talk to you about the need for specialty crossing operators, mainly because we breathe, work the border and eat and sleep the border, if you will, every single day. You'll also find that we are probably the most significant partners in both fostering security and trade that you will find.

I want to just as a background let you know that we view security as——

Mr. SOUDER. Mr. Mayer, could you just—I know this is still confusing to me from time to time, but explain how you're different from Customs and Border Patrol. A lot of times people think you're all the same unit.

Mr. MAYER. Sure. And I'm—very quickly.

First of all, the crossing operators, we're a unique creation, the bridge tunnel operators which I'm also the president, there are nine crossings; eight bridge authorities and one tunnel operation. We are all different. Some of us are compact organizations of the U.S. Constitution, some of us are both State agencies, State and provincial agencies, one of us is private.

The tunnel, for example, is owned by two cities and operated by a private investment bank. So we are unique creations that I should also point out that Customs and Immigration, all the Federal law enforcement agencies are tenants of ours. We own the facility and provide them for the Federal agencies. There's no direct Federal role, either the United States or Canada in the border crossings, other than the inspection operation.

My theme that I want to make this morning is as follows; economic security and physical security have to be in balance. We cannot have one without the other. The second is, and I just talked to you briefly about it, the bridge tunnel operators you will find are very, very helpful and important partners in this entire effort to improve physical security, economic security of our countries. And finally, I want to also talk very briefly about the issue of leadership. When you go around the country and you hold these committees, I think you hear from a group of people all pretty much saying the same thing.

So what we're seeing now is a real need for and it's coming from committees such as this, for leadership to define the border of tomorrow. I'll talk very quickly about that in a moment. Let me give you some little background. The nine major crossings all located over the contributory waterways, the Great Lakes Basin, handle 75 percent of all Canada-U.S. trade; over $750 million every single day in merchandise trade. And we've been doing that successfully for many, many years.

With the exception of the Bluewater Bridge which was built in 1997, the second span of the Bluewater, no new infrastructures capacity has been built on the northern border, bridges, tunnel infrastructure, with the exception of the Lewiston-Queenston Bridge in 1962, yet trade has burgeoned and ballooned over those crossings going back to the auto pact agreement in the 1960's, free trade in the 1980's, and the NAFTA in the 1990's and has been possible for two ways.

Through technology, and improved practices at the border by all the Federal inspection agencies. That won't last forever. We need major infrastructural expansion, bridge and border expansion, we also need improved connecting road networks coming to them.

In a post September 11th world, one of the things that's coming to stark reality, national security interests, physical and economic security interests, have now gone head long into local land use and jurisdictional issues. To add new capacity at the border now in any meaningful way is a 10 to 15 year effort. I suggest to you we simply cannot wait that long.

Here's a few recommendations, you've heard some of them today. Prearrival processing system. No commercial carriers should enter our country without transmitting documents ahead of time; it does three things. No. 1, let's us know what's coming. No. 2, it improves—so that improves physical security. No. 2, it facilitates trade because trucks aren't sitting at the border getting their documents in order. No. 3, goods in motion are more secure and pollute less than goods sitting at the border—than trucks sitting at the border.

The second is the issue of flexible processing. Legislation such as Public Law 108–7, we're beginning to look at better ways to manage the border of tomorrow and create the border of tomorrow. We also support a rapid expansion of money for Federal agencies for IT architecture, that costs amongst agencies and also you heard it from Customs before, we really need a automated commercial manifest for commercial carriers. In this day and age we really shouldn't be using those paper manifests for trucks coming to our border.

And finally, the economic piece, border crossings work because the connections too and from them work. So we believe in the next round of authorizations of what is now TEA–21, that a very hard and coordinated look needs to be taken at how goods and people move too and from our border. Thank you very much.

Mr. SOUDER. Thank you.

Mr. Rich is representing Dr. Rudnick, is that correct?

STATEMENT OF LUKE RICH, SENIOR CONSULTANT, BUFFALO NIAGARA PARTNERSHIP

Mr. RICH. Correct. My name is Luke Rich. I am senior consultant with the Buffalo Niagara Partnership which is an upstate New York's largest business organization. Dr. Rudnick unfortunately was indisposed at the last minute this morning, so I'd like to present his statement.

I want to focus in on the topic of border security and leave you one very simple, very important message. Something that has become a sort of mantra for many of us in the business community: Border Security Can Equal Border Efficiency.

What does that mean? That means that as we all look for the ways to tighten border security as a result of the horrific events of September 11, we must be sure that the actions we take at the border do not harm the movement of goods or people between the United States and Canada and where possible, actually improves this commerce.

Consider that in 2001, Canada bought more goods from the United States than all the European Union countries combined; three times more than Japan and 61 percent more than Mexico. The United States exports more than $250 billion in goods to Canada each year and more than 30 percent of that commerce crosses the bridges here in western New York.

There was a time when many of us thought that an open border between Canada and United States was a real possibility. It may still be possible. However, it will only happen if our two countries can agree on ways to secure the North American Perimeter, thus, relieving pressure on the over 5,000 mile border between our two countries. This goal can be achieved, but not in the immediate future. None-the-less border security and border efficiency are not mutually exclusive.

That's why numerous business and trade organizations from across New York have met to form the New York State Smart Border Coalition. Our goal is to advocate for a policy that ensures the secure free flow of goods and people and services at the various crossing points between New York State and Canada.

This can only be achieved by expediting the flow of low risk goods and people so that customs and immigration officials in both countries can concentrate on those they don't know, who may be a greater risk to our security. Minister Manley and Secretary Ridge and their staff are doing an excellent job in this regard. In fact of the 30 points in their game plan for a safe and secure border, major progress has been achieved in all but two points.

It is the issue of joint inspection, reverse inspection, creation of international zones that I want to call your particular attention today. These three terms represent different ways of achieving the same end. It is vital to the bridge and tunnel crossings in western New York and Michigan, where over 70 percent of the Canadian American trade crosses, those customs inspectors be able to do their job in each other's country.

These bridges and tunnels are vital to the economic security of our two nations. Millions of jobs in virtually every State and province depend on keeping these crossings open. Thirty-eight U.S. States have Canada as their largest trading partner. The expansion of capacity, security, expedition of trade and travel across these bridges and tunnels is a national issue, not a local issue. If you take nothing away from this hearing other than that, we have made our point.

Here in western New York, millions of dollars can be saved and years of delay avoided in the construction of inspection plazas, if U.S. Customs can do their inspections in Fort Erie, Ontario after the new Peace Bridge is constructed.

Progress in the negotiations between Canada Customs and U.S. Customs is painfully slow. You, the Congress of the United States have passed legislation permitting Customs to negotiate an agreement. You have also passed legislation calling for a pilot project at the Peace Bridge. However, it appears the negotiators are bogged down on the issues of procedure, which have already been, at least partially resolved with the airport inspection agreement signed between the two countries in 2002.

What is needed is for negotiations to move to the highest level of each government in order to overcome the inertia of traditional procedures and hypothetical worst case scenarios. Continued pressure from you will be enormously important. We cannot allow the largest trade and tourism relationship in the world to be jeopardized by the reluctance of bureaucrats to give up traditional ways. Thank you for your attention.

Mr. SOUDER. Thank you.

Before yielding to Congressman Shadegg for questions, let me first explain the kind of good and bad news of what's happened here. We had no idea how many Members were going to come to this hearing. And whenever you have more Members, the questions of the earlier panels takes longer.

If you're going to make tonight's votes, you have to leave a few minutes ago, actually probably hopefully they'll make their plane. Congressman Shadegg and I decided to skip votes tonight so we're here. Congresswoman Slaughter was particularly upset because she would have except she has a Rules meeting at 5 o'clock that she also needed to be at. She wanted to make sure that it got on the record what her particular extra pressure was. And this is kind of her district, you're her direct people and it's been particularly upsetting in this process with that. But she had been checking to see if she could miss the Rules meeting and she really couldn't.

Each of the Members expressed their frustration. But the good news is we have had a lot of people here. The other thing is Congressman Shadegg—well, actually, a couple of—in reorganizing how the Federal Government is going to try to deal with homeland security and if you figure it out before us, let us know. [Laughter.]

We are working through a very difficult process, it's very hard for some agencies to figure out how to do that. But what we know is the general publics tolerance is zero if we fail, but impatient if we impede commerce, which is actually the No. 1 issue involved. In trying to balance these two things it has been very difficult. Well, in addition to the two committees, the Border Subcommittee of the Homeland Security which Congressman Shadegg and I both serve, and this drug policy which has had oversight over all these different agencies, Congressman Shadegg Chairs the Subcommittee on the Emergency Response and Preparedness and the Intelligence equipment, the technology as well.

So that subcommittee wasn't part of this today but he's the chairman of that and I'm on that subcommittee too. So we're all wearing multiple hats so we wanted to stay and make sure we heard from all of you today. Now I'll yield to Congressman Shadegg.

Mr. SHADEGG. Thank you, Mr. Chairman. And I'll start with a round of questions if I may—usually when you ask questions I'm provoked to ask others because you stimulate my curiosity. But let me start with a few, Mr. Mayer, let me start with you. I'm intrigued with your concept of the border of tomorrow. I am particularly interested, Congressman Souder mentioned that my subcommittee within Homeland Security has not only emergency preparedness and response, but also as he indicated technology.

Mark and I, actually, I think the year we were first elected went to the border at Nogales and looked at what was then the cutting edge technology at a new commercial crossing center they had there for commercial trucks crossing the Arizona-Mexico border coming into Mexico. And it was state-of-the-art at the time. But I think that was 7 years ago, Mark? I'm sure it was.

I would like you to describe for me kind of the key elements of the border of tomorrow, both from the commercial standpoint and from a civilian tourist standpoint. And if you would, focus on any technology that you are aware of or you think we ought be looking at with particular emphasis on homeland security issues.

Mr. MAYER. Thank you, Congressman. First of all, let me—when I talk about the border of tomorrow, I'm not only talking about a line on a map, I think the border extends right to the factory door. It extends to the individual that's leaving their house in the morning and has their NEXUS card and they're going to cross into another country. It focuses first on what I'll call preparedness.

And it allows Federal agencies in particular to make sure that their resources go to—their resources are focused on the high risk traveler and high risk commercial carrier. And the 90 plus percent that are doing what they should be are on the programs and technologies such as FAST, NCAP, and they're CEPAT compliant, and that whole other world of acronyms. And they provide them other things such as transponder technology. For example, the Peace Bridge uses electronic toll collections in our tolling operations and we're part of the E-Zpass the inter-agency group in the northeast. And that—those transponders, in fact, new technologies coming out allow a lot more information than just toll collections to go on there; information on the goods, the traveler and all that. So that's part of the technology.

Also another thing I think it's necessary to make the border work, between Canada and United States so much of our economic security rests in interfirm and intrafirm industry trade. So the border crossings now are part and parcel of the manufacturing system. A bridge now is literally part of an assembly line. One of the things the crossing operators have been talking, we have all gone out and done independent threat assessments of our infrastructure. Working with Transport Canada, the U.S.'s counterpart of the U.S. Department of Transportation, we have taken all our individual threat assessments and hammered out with Transport Canada leadership, the best management practices to infrastructure security.

A key part of that is regional mobility. For example, what happens if the Ambassador Bridge went out of a service, in a real threat, something actually happened? How would we route that critical traffic in that area? The same if you're in the Niagara region. So that's part of it too. It's that whole region mobility planning at and around international crossings as well.

For example, I mean, I know that the Brooklyn Bridge and the—for example, the Golden Gate Bridge are national icons. But I can assure you, if you want to create serious disruption in North America, if the Ambassador Bridge were lost or the Peace Bridge, the economic consequences would be disastrous.

Mr. SHADEGG. You indicated that you performed a threat assessment. Is that threat assessment shared or has it been shared with the Bureau of Immigration and Customs Enforcement or the Bureau of Customs Enforcement Protection?

Mr. MAYER. We have shared that threat assessment with FHWA, their office of Critical Bridge Infrastructure. The bridge operators have a seat at the table of FHWAs Blue Ribbon Committee on security. We're not a voting member but we've been asked to participate and sit in. And this Friday I have a meeting in Washington with Under Secretary Asa Hutchinson and it's one of the issues that we'll be discussing.

Mr. SHADEGG. Mr. Feely, I was fascinated by some parts of information as a dedicated need to a great degree and I was unaware of this COBRA fund or its inclusion in the Senate and the House version that may get resolved yet this week. And I think it is our leadership intention to pass that legislation this week. That is completely user fee funded?

Mr. FEELY. The COBRA Fund is, yes.

Mr. SHADEGG. And it is used simply to pay for overtime?

Mr. FEELY. No. Well, during a fall-off in funding for the agency in earlier years, it initially started as a fund to fund overtime. But we actually began to use it as I mentioned 1,200 positions, through the last authorization, were paid for out of the COBRA fund. That's complete salaries, expenses, benefits, everything.

Mr. SHADEGG. So that's going to actual personnel?

Mr. FEELY. Yes. We're using that as a funding mechanism to provide personnel at the borders, so if it's not reauthorized, then we're going to have to pick up the cost for those 1,200 people that are currently just doing a regular 8 hour day who are picked up on COBRA's Fund.

Mr. SOUDER. I want to move to a separate line of questions so I don't have to raise that question. Do you know was it just not focused on in the House, was there an opposition of the funds?

Mr. FEELY. I'm not certain. I can give you a contact points with NT's national office who are actually lobbying up on the Hill. We're not certain why this was—it wasn't included in any legislation in the House. But, I mean, it's an issue that we have been raising, NTU has been raising for the last 2 years because we knew it would have an impact on our funding capabilities.

Mr. SHADEGG. Pardon my ignorance, but I'm going to try to wade through this and try to understand some points here. You represent Treasury Employees, which means you represent—when I deal with Customs Agents on the border at Mexico, you would represent them?

Mr. FEELY. Yes.

Mr. SHADEGG. That would include Customs Agents that do the open border between ports and also Customs Agents at the port, is that correct?

Mr. FEELY. Well, the way it stands right now we're dealing in terms of legacy agencies. I, myself, am a Customs Inspector assigned here to the four bridges in Buffalo and Niagara Falls. In a sense Custom serves as part of the Treasury Department, we became part of the National Treasury Employees Union.

Now, there are Legacy Immigration Naturalization Service Officers and there are Legacy Border Patrol Officers, they belong to the American Federation of Government employees. They get their representation through them. In a sense, I represent everybody, I can speak for everybody because I worked side-by-side with the Immigration Inspectors at the border crossing points.

This is—just as the Government is trying to deal with the combination of 22 agencies, there's been a problem for Federal unions. We are now trying to deal with a combination of all these different employees who are represented by in particular two different unions. And the Annual Plan Health Inspection Service inspectors have their own union.

Mr. SHADEGG. I guess the point I want to get to is, you make a plea for law enforcement officer status. And as I've indicated previously, and Mark indicated previously, we are on the—I was on the Arizona-Mexico border at a gate recently where I talked with some Customs employees; and with Mark I was on the Tohono O'odham Indian Reservation when we stopped at some customs agents and they actually showed us around.

They clearly—those agents were clearly performing law enforcement functions. They are carrying weapons, they are dealing with more dangerous border crossers on the southern border than Border Patrol is. The Border Patrol is largely dealing with human traffic, most of which are crossing the southern border simply looking for a job. They want to come to the United States because the economy in Mexico will not sustain them, many of them come across alone, get a job here and send money across the border.

If they are apprehended, they make generally no opposition. They are simply apprehended, and Mark and I were watching and they were just grabbed, they're put on a bus, they're sent right back across the border and the next night they cross again. They do not pose a very serious threat anywhere near as serious as a threat to life as do the drug smugglers, that Mark and I also encountered on that same trip. What I want to understand about if this is what your testimony is, are you telling me that those Customs Agents that we met, who patrol the borders for drug smugglers, are currently not law enforcement certified?

Mr. FEELY. No. Are you referring to the members of the Immigration Custom Enforcement Branch now?

Mr. SHADEGG. Apparently so.

Mr. FEELY. Yeah. The agents that work for the Bureau of Immigration of Custom Enforcement are law enforcement trained.

Mr. SHADEGG. And so your plea here is for what specifically?

Mr. FEELY. Custom and Border Patrol Inspectors who are now comparable—comprised of the Legacy Custom Inspectors, Immigration Inspectors and——

Mr. SHADEGG. Who would be at ports?

Mr. FEELY. We work at the ports of entry.

Mr. SHADEGG. OK. Thank you. Mark, that's all I have at this point.

Mr. SOUDER. I first wanted to make two references to Mr. Mayer's testimony. One, is on your point nine, where you mention about the Northern Border Congressional Caucus. Two of the three recommendations that came out of groups at the Interparliamentary Conference would reduce some long term regular dialog between United States and Canada to try to head off some of the different problems. So I'm not sure, they pointed out that 10 years ago they similarly resolved that, so we're trying to figure out how to coordinate with the executive branch committee between the House and Senate there. And I believe there's going to be more effort because there's more consciousness about the border right now.

The most disturbing thing that you had in your testimony and I'm still trying to figure out, is that you have a point six: U.S. Federal agencies should review security plans, practices and procedures at each crossing and provide expert input into the planning. The goal here is to maintain the best practices approach to infrastructure security.

Are you telling me that currently the Federal agencies don't look at any security regarding the bridges, your plans or anything?

Mr. MAYER. Not as much as I think that they could and provide the input. We obviously, as the owners of that infrastructure, make sure that we're protecting that infrastructure, reviewing it and putting in place a whole host of security measures. The intent of point six was really to say, as the Federal Government, either through FHWA or Homeland Security sees potential gaps that might exist in what we term critical infrastructure, that they work with the crossing operators to point that out, such that we can always make sure that we're at the leading edge of where we want to be in protecting our infrastructure. And also alerting us, making sure that we're always alerted to potential threats as well.

Mr. SOUDER. Let's say hypothetically that there was a case at one—which bridge are you again?

Mr. MAYER. Peace Bridge.

Mr. SOUDER. At the Peace Bridge, like what happened at Ambassador where the people with suspicious packages may have not been enough to warn the Ambassador Bridge that they were intercepted a couple weeks ago. How does this work, do you have guards there to intercept, the Federal Government happened to come in because they had a specific tip where they called in; how would it work in your case or how does that interrelate with the local Sheriff? Are they tipped off? There's a specific example. How does that work here in Buffalo?

Mr. MAYER. Well, let me—first of all, as a Peace Bridge employee, I should point out we have 100 employees that work for the Peace Bridge Authority. If you put all the Federal agencies and the trade community people there, over 1,000 people work at the Peace Bridge. We are not law enforcement. We do not have law enforcement procedures or authority.

Mr. SOUDER. You're more structural questions on security, not protecting it from a bomber?

Mr. MAYER. We're both. For example, we get bomb scares all the time. I shouldn't say all the time, we might get one or two a year. Someone will call, for example, when Sheik Rachman was convicted, we'll get a call that, "I've planted a bomb on your structure." So what happens is it comes to us, we the Peace Bridge have a call from a law enforcement agency, be it the city of Buffalo Police, or the Regional Police, because frankly the only one who knows what should be on the structure is ourselves because we own and operate the structure.

So we will go out with them, if we deem it a credible threat we talk to Customs, Customs Officials now Homeland Security, the former Customs Officials and Immigration, close down the booths and we close the bridge; if we deem it to be a credible threat. We then notify what's called NITTEC, which is a group of transportation agents in the area that send messages out to all the transportation agencies that the Peace Bridge is closed, that we have travel advisory radio, there will be variable messages through the New York Thruway. We call our colleagues at the Niagara Falls Bridge and say we are sending all of our traffic to you.

That's the general procedure that takes place right now. I think it could be a bit better coordinated, not only in the Niagara region but what would happen, for example, if severe disruption happened in the Niagara region that might effect the Lewiston-Queenston Bridge? Would the vehicles move say to the St. Lawrence region to cross?

I think we need to take a little bit broader look at the mobility—as I talked about before, the mobility in the area, that is No. 1. And specific to the bridge itself, what we're asking just when Federal agencies may be looking at state-of-the-art techniques, via camera monitoring, remote sensing, that they work with the crossing operators. You will find us—if you called us up and say we want all nine of you crossing operators in Washington tomorrow, we will all be there. You will find us very good partners.

Mr. SOUDER. If we check or random check truckers going over, cars going over, Federal employees, people who work on the bridge do you have a screening procedure?

Mr. MAYER. We haven't in the past. It's something we're looking at right now. But as to what we can do, we're a unionized work environment so there's certain obviously protections there that we have to make sure that we follow. But if just look at the Federal agencies, as it was discussed earlier, at the radiation portal monitors, auto licensed plate readers, and a whole range of technologies to check the people and the goods coming in.

But I'm not only talking about that, I'm talking about someone who might want to approach our piers from the Niagara River or land side and do damage to our structure. Now, we're doing a lot to do take care of that. Crossing operators on their own are doing that. My issue there is, more as the Federal Government might see best practices or changing trends in technology that might help us, that they make us aware.

Mr. SOUDER. This has been a big issue at airports.

Mr. MAYER. Certainly.

Mr. SOUDER. People who are—I mean, they screen everybody through but if you're not checking the people who do the repairs on the airplanes or who are moving around at the airports, what was the point of screening all the passengers who are going over the bridge and I just wondered what the extent of that was.

Sheriff, it was interesting your anecdotal stories about finding immigrants walking around and the little boy, which still are exceptions not in the rule. But what do you—how would you describe other than frustration and some good days, the interrelationship that you have right now and how your working relationship with the Border Patrol and Customs and DEA and the other agencies? Have you seen a somewhat of an increase in their ability to work with you, a lot of increase?

Mr. BEILEIN. I would describe it as good to excellent. I think one of the great accomplishments since September 11 was the creation of the Joint Terrorism Task Forces and involving local law enforcement in that task force. It's been a good accomplishment and I mentioned in my testimony that it has to be—you have to have certain ingredients, you have to have dedicated officers and you also have to have the leadership and the resources. And I think that the Federal Government needs to supply those leadership and those resources.

But the communications between myself and the Coast Guard that you had up here earlier, the Border Patrol up there, has been very, very good. It was never bad, however, since the World Trade Centers terrorist attacks it has improved dramatically and this reaches across the border to my Canadian counterparts in law enforcement.

Mr. SOUDER. So if one of you moved toward, there's somebody that shouldn't be moving in that location or there's an object of suspicion, do you have a pretty good fast interconnect now, because you may have—unlike the southern border, where there are Border Patrol people everywhere, not everywhere but lots more than on the north and that's why your people are often at those points in the gaps. And they see something, first to be able to respond, is it almost instantaneous or is there a bounce back delay?

Mr. BEILEIN. I believe there's a small bounce back delay, we don't have the interoperability with our computer systems with the Federal Government.

Mr. SOUDER. Do you use RIIDS or any of those?

Mr. BEILEIN. No. I think in the case—I hate to go back to the 7-year-old boy but it took some good questioning by local law enforcement of that 7 year-old to determine that he did cross the border. And it wasn't until he mentioned a particular school that he went to that it was realized that he crossed the border. A lot of it depends on the instinct and training of the local law enforcement officer when he encounters that type of situation.

Mr. SOUDER. I want to ask a question with Ms. Hamilton and—related to see how you might have in your local Sheriff's Office, I'm trying to understand some of the concept of what you're saying. Let me first put it in laymens terms and give you an example in my district and then see how this fits. You're proposing that this information overlay be on one of your broad band signals?

Ms. HAMILTON. Yes. We are assigned one broadband but you can send different bits of information at the same time.

Mr. SOUDER. And would this be open information to everyone if they bought one of those receivers or would it be just for law enforcement?

Ms. HAMILTON. It is very secure. A receiver you can buy at Radioshack. These tuner cards are specially programmed and they have a special mechanism to decrypt. So as an example, even if there was information you wanted to share with Erie County Sheriff's Department but—or Niagara County Sheriff's Department but you do not want the Health Department knowing it, you can address the information to exactly who you want to receive it. And unless somebody has the proper tuner card, they cannot receive the information.

Mr. SOUDER. Sheriff, in one of the counties that I represent has a more advanced systems that I've seen they have a computer hookup that's gradually been putting in by building and block, they're increasing getting the blueprint plans in, so that for example, when a—although it's Homeland Security, when a tornado approached from one angle, they could actually tell people which side of the building to move through and they can also for fires and rescue purposes be able to track that. Do you have a similar thing here?

Mr. BEILEIN. We have a basic computer system. I think what I was referring to was being able to access the Federal data bases, for instance, for illegal immigrants that we happen to see walking down the road, which is usually the case. But as far as an overall computer system, yes, we're tied in with——

Mr. SOUDER. But do you have a mapping technique for your county that shows you where the houses are, with blueprints? I know it's relatively new because it's a new technology.

Mr. BEILEIN. That is in the next round of the cops grants that's coming down to purchase that, with the mapping and so forth.

Mr. SOUDER. How do you see that type of program overlapping?

Ms. HAMILTON. Well, public broadcasting is just a distribution mechanism. But I think what we offer is to see—and I'll give you an example, I was speaking with someone from the Upper Mountain Fire Co. and they said they do have maps and data bases of critical sites in their area, if there's a bio-hazard from some sort of terrorist threats. They have this information but the other fire companies that may be responding do not have this information. It would be very cumbersome under ordinary circumstances to get this information to all of the first responders from all the different agencies.

Now, with our system it can be set up and distributed to them almost simultaneously. It eliminates the lag. I don't know how long the lag is now in terms of information sharing or getting access to the Federal Government, the advantage of this system is that once the information is set up, we can get it out almost instantaneously.

Mr. SOUDER. Well, one of the things that we should look at because one of the problems is that if a city—if the city's inside a county and the city cooperates, you all can't get on the same systems and get these new kind of technologies so there's no lag. But what a TV—regional approach does is help us address a couple potential questions.

One is, the cities and counties in some places tend to argue at times over jurisdiction. It's been known to happen in many States. Furthermore, different counties are known to not necessarily want the same system. And if you're—when you're an individual, even for tornadoes, but certainly if it was some kind of an attack coming, you don't want to have one set of information depending on trying to figure out where the county line is, the township line is here, the city here, because the annex of this block could have a whole different evacuation plan. And trying to force that intergration, one may be the way the data is communicated. It's something we need to look at as we evolve.

Mr. SHADEGG. If I could interrupt. Let me just ask you Ms. Hamilton, I understand that you're proposing this for an information—as an information link for first responders. Are you familiar with an organization called America's 911?

Ms. HAMILTON. No, I'm not.

Mr. SHADEGG. I have constituents who helped develop this and it's a computer link that has been set up, it's set up across the country, it's being much more broadly used and currently the Homeland Security Department is in discussion with them. But they serve as a single point of information for information sought by individuals.

For example, there's tons of information that EPA generates on how clean a given beach is but they don't know how to get it out. You drive into the town, you can call this number but if you go to the next town you have to call a different number. They have an entire system where literally all of these agencies up-link their data to a single source and you can go on and you put in your disk and it will tell you how clean the beach is at the various beaches that are close to you or further away from you. And it goes on and on and on. And they're currently up-linking this. I guess one question I have—I have two questions for you.

One, is the proposal that you made to us written up in a written form to submit to Congress or to submit to the Homeland Security Department or the Select Committee on Homeland Security, which Mark and I serve? I'd be interested if it's not, in having you do that and get us a copy. And second, have you given thought, since as you pointed out this could be a quick link for to get information quickly to all of the first responders in the areas. Have you looked to a parallel system that would get information out to computer data bases or computers for the general population?

Ms. HAMILTON. We do have a trade organization in public broadcasting called APTS, which is based in Washington, DC, and they do have complete information. And in fact, if you would like a live demonstration of this, they would be glad to provide one to you. In terms of information sharing, we're a distribution mechanism. It would be up to the governmental agency to determine how we use this information mechanism to the benefits of the agencies, the first responders, local and State governments and also governments on both sides of the border.

It could be used for any application. I mean, if the time came that you want to use emergency bands or someone in the Defense Department for whatever reason to talk to everyone in the public, I mean, it's public airways. And I think the advantage for first responders is to bridge the gap between Washington and Buffalo and Niagara Falls and Toronto and Fort Erie and among different agencies.

First responders may have a very good communication network but do they have a connection to the CDC if there is a bio-hazard information. I think a really good example is when the SARS scare came out, it took 2 to 3 days for all hospitals to find out what the symptoms were, how you should handle the situation. With this system, CDC could have sent up the information and it could have been broadcast by public broadcasting stations to all hospitals that just had this tuner card. And if you have a LAN system which most hospitals do, you'd need one card for an entire system.

Mr. SHADEGG. I have a couple other questions for a few other witnesses. I wanted to ask the Sheriff, I was fascinated with your testimony regarding the kind of smuggling routes that are known, some of which have been around since prohibition, and we have those problems on the Mexico border. On our latest trip down there they took us to the top of the peak that sits right on the border and the drug smugglers will send a lookout to the top of that peak with a clear view to the south, clear view to the north, and they'll sit there with a little radio and he can sit on top of that peek with a pair of binoculars and look for miles east and know whether there are any agents anywhere around. And if there are, he radios his people and says, stay put or if he looks and doesn't see anybody he says come on through.

So I guess I'm interested in any thoughts you have on how do you deal with the unique water problems you have. How do you deal with those or is it simply, we're going to have that level of smuggling no matter what we do when you have an open water like this or like what I have, an open desert——

Mr. BEILEIN. It's a difficult situation to deal with. You can't patrol the water of Lake Ontario like we patrol the highway and the fact that with the speed of boats and so forth today, you can go from the heart of Toronto to any one of those inlets in a matter of 30 minutes or less, depending on the speed of the boats. I think it's something that both sides has to work on to stop it on the other side before it gets here. And we have to continue to be vigilant. I don't see a situation like in the Bahama line where you're putting up blimps and radar type of devices in order to detect boats crossing the open water, but what I see is a stepped up intelligence gathering and stepped up information on the people who are doing the smuggling. I believe it doesn't just happen with drugs, it happens with people too.

I have had the experience of fishing people out of water dead. A Malaysian national tried to cross the water in January and was found dead in the water and those situations where you're talking about at the most half an hour to be on the other side of the lake and into the United States.

Mr. SHADEGG. I wish you luck. I know our border in the desert is a real challenge. One last question for you Mr. Deveso. You heard the testimony about the COBRA user fee imposed on your commercial vehicles, I am safe to assume that you as an industry representative don't have a problem with that user fee and those kinds of efforts to help fund say the border of the future, a border that is operable, that ports are secure, but also commercially viable? Is that something you're supportive of or are there problems here?

Mr. DEVESO. Any user fee implemented, if the purpose for which the money is derived goes for the purpose of its accomplishment, we have no problem. The problem is most user fees facing the trucking industries is the misappropriation of funds. That being said, we have no problem whatsoever if it's a matter of national security.

What you have to go look out for and I'm going to get away from your question a little bit, is the passing on of the costs of lost time during these crisis times. And it's not even if you're paying drivers, for example, by the hour, there's a—there's stress factors involved and related costs to driver retention and companies having the ability to waiting to be crossing the borders.

Mr. SOUDER. You want a trust fund that is secure, like Social Security?

Mr. SHADEGG. I'll point out, the user fees on one hand look very attractive. But shouldn't the people take the—on the other hand I'll tell you my brother and I have had an ongoing discussion on the issue and so forth of parks user fees. But he makes a point of saying, John, I pay my general taxes and to pay to go into those parks, why should I have to pay a user fee on top of those, we don't make others in our society who get government services to pay a user fee. And one could construct an agreement to the fact that to secure our borders, whether be it for—from drugs or terrorism or just make them operate well commercially, that is a general good and it's not necessarily just a good that is used by the people who cross the borders all the time. So before we'd elect to go to Congress—I thought user fees were a no brainer and I discovered since then they're a little more complicated.

Mr. DEVESO. I agree, when you're going from private sector to commercial, it's more complicated being that operating ratios, those costs also eventually are passed down in the private pocket sector.

Mr. SHADEGG. Absolutely. Thank you.

Mr. SOUDER. It's amazing how many industries because of their frustration at this slow speed of the Federal bureaucracy, are going to these different fees to do that. I met with egg producers the other day and they can't process their egg proceeds so they're willing to take a fee in order to get the FDA and all sorts of things. That is why if you know it can be used and dedicated to that fund, in fact, that is where the conflict is.

Mr. DEVESO. The disadvantage is our user taxes and fees in New York State are the highest in the country, so we have a problem here aside from the Federal standards.

Mr. SOUDER. I have two trucking questions. One, is we run into this at the ports more with ships and we heard from some of the shippers, let me yield with the first question. As we deal with the FAST pass entry and all these different challenges, the question comes who is going to be held accountable in the challenge with the truck—the trucking company which have an independent driver, the cab owner may not be the same as the trailer and they may or may not know who loaded it or something could be attached to it?

We've had testimony that they would be willing to have higher penalties if somebody abused that, but the question comes first off, how do we sort out a practical line of responsibilities because it isn't going to work for each part to say it was the others responsibilities?

Mr. DEVESO. I'm not sure I have an answer to that question. Right now in New York State we're initiating FAST now and it's—the way I understand the system, by educating the industry itself and raising that level of confidence right from the origin to the destination, including the trucking company, including the driver, I would agree with those constituents that they would raise the bar on penalty. Because of that level of confidential, the higher the penalty should be.

Mr. SOUDER. Would you have that be on whoever's name is on the truck or who the designated driver is?

Mr. DEVESO. Unfortunately, where the system is right now, the conveyance—one, the product is loaded on the conveyance of distribution at interstate commerce, unfortunately it falls on the trucker.

Mr. SOUDER. One other truck question. I was in the furniture retailing business and when we'd get furniture on a truck, we'd get a bill of lading, then you got a more specific invoice. Part of the debate in how we can do monitoring is that the bills of lading are what—are generally be checked in at our customs and ports. I'm not sure how the trucking works, in other words, they get a general description of a box with chairs or maybe even two chairs and the invoice says French provincial yellow, such and such. A lot of people want to wait until the last minute to put the specifics of what's inside and what that means in the monitoring is that there isn't necessarily a match and therefore it doesn't—what some of the trucking companies are arguing is because the people who are loading their trucks aren't being specific enough about what's coming in, it may not be fair to hold them accountable because we're asking for the wrong information.

Mr. DEVESO. I disagree with them. I think they should be held accountable. Dealing with LTD split shipments, varying shipments, container shipments, probably are the most difficult. I think if the seamless process has to be accomplished or could be accomplished, it would have to be done because the level of confidence would have to be raised at the point of origin, the shipper, the person loading the vehicle. Then it goes on to the conveyance and on to the person receiving the product. And if everything were to be perfected the way it's supposed to be and in reaching more than 50 percent expectation that were discussed earlier, I think beyond 50 percent, you could have a seamless way.

Mr. SOUDER. So you believe in the trucking area the paper you're currently providing is accurate enough to be measured in accountability?

Mr. DEVESO. It's accurate enough to ornate the paperwork. But if there's a level of confidence from the source, knowing and understanding that shipping document and then passing it forward and then processing it over the computer system, then they could be adequate.

Mr. SOUDER. Thanks. I want to tell Mr. Rich, we always try to include the business sector in the testimony, although you may not get as much cross. But to make sure all records show when we plunge into the details of trying to figure out security, we don't forget the trade question. Would you like to add anything?

Mr. RICH. First, on the user fee issue, the general business community is not adverse to user fees as long as they are not used for substitution for others. I think if I understood the testimony earlier, 1,200 people are being paid out of users fees, so we would have an objection to that as a business community.

Mr. SOUDER. And what if they're lost?

Mr. RICH. We think they should be—if we need 1,200 people, they should be paid the same way the other however many thousands that are there are. That of course throws the ball back in your court, but if it's a priority, it should be a priority. If the user fee is for some further level of security, that would be fine. The other issue is on the question of the future. There's a NEXUS pass now, there's work toward some sort of a secure frequent flyer kind of pass, there's also some work toward something with cruise ships. All three systems are, as far as we understand, different and incompatible. And it makes no sense if we're going to have a pass, let's have a pass we can use everywhere.

Mr. SOUDER. If you get a copy of this report, that's one of the criticisms we issued. They were testing too many systems. That is one of the things John's subcommittee will be focusing in on. I mean, this is ridiculous. I mean, if they can't talk to each other, this is just silliness and the first terrorist that gets through because we didn't synchronize our system, some heads will roll.

Mr. RICH. I think the Federal regulations are contributing to that too. They are testing different systems——

Mr. SOUDER. Partly. Now we have more dollars to invest in that. In fairness to the agencies, they are trying to piece together what next but now it's crunch time. The other thing you can kind of hear, the problem in the north border and south border are substantially different. One of the differences is on the north border we have peak times that jam or when a problem occurs they jam because it's over water, so you have bridge structure problems. And we're used to just in time delivery.

On the south borders they have back-ups all the time, at El Paso, Laredo. We have—they don't just have the peak back-ups at certain times, Sunday nights and that type of thing or holiday periods as it can happen in the north. They got it all the time on the south. It's almost like they factor it in, but they're frustrated because obviously the cities just north of the south border Los Angeles, Phoenix, San Diego, Houston, Dallas and the pressure is on us to address some of the questions and the differences between the borders.

With the new president of Mexico, we're making progress, the trucking standards are different in Mexico than Canada, the training regulations are different. I'm not saying you don't have these, but these are huge political challenges to us and a hearing like today is helpful because we have both north and south border people here arguing. I don't have any border crossing but trying to reconcile some of this on a national priority, you've got to hear some of that. And what we want to do is make sure in the north, in a place where we for the most part haven't thought—even admitting Canada is a different country, is a real challenge for us as opposed to cultural and language difficulties. As we work, we have to be fair if Canada—if Mexico was proposing drug policy changes like Canada, Congress would be going ballistic. And that's going to come up if they do that because we would react so strongly on the Mexican border and there's going to be equity questions, so we're working hard to work through these things. And I thought personally the most interesting statistic was there was nothing new in the north border other than the Bluewater Bridge. Did that count any lane additions?

Mr. MAYER. A three lane bridge that opened in 1997.

Mr. SOUDER. Thank you very much for your patience today and your testimony.

[Whereupon, the subcommittees adjourned.]

[Additional information submitted for the hearing record follows:]

U.S. Department of Justice

Drug Enforcement Administration

Washington, D.C. 20537

JUL 29 2003

The Honorable Mark Souder
Chairman, Subcommittee on Criminal Justice,
Drug Policy and Human Resources
2157 Rayburn House Office Building
Washington, D.C. 20515

Re: Improving Security and Facilitating Commerce at the Northern Border:
Field Hearing in Niagara Falls, New York

Dear Chairman Souder:

This is in response to questions submitted by the Subcommittee on Criminal Justice, Drug Policy and Human Resources based upon the testimony of Associate Special Agent in Charge (A/SAC) William J. Walker of the Drug Enforcement Administration's New York Field Division. A/SAC Walker appeared before the Government Reform Subcommittee on Criminal Justice, Drug Policy and Human Resources Field Hearing in Niagara Falls, New York on May 19, 2003.

Enclosed are the responses to the follow-up questions provided for the hearing record. If I can be of further assistance, please do not hesitate to contact me.

Sincerely,

William B. Simpkins
Acting Administrator

Enclosure

NORTHERN BORDER FIELD HEARING
May 19, 2003
Questions for the Record

Drug Enforcement Administration (DEA)

1. What has been the specific impact of U.S.-Canadian cross-border law enforcement ventures such as Project Northstar and the IBET teams? What concrete results have they had? Could these initiatives be improved?

In summary, both Project Northstar (PNS) and the Integrated Border Enforcement Teams (IBETs) served to formalize relationships as well as the sharing of resources and intelligence between municipal, county, state, and federal law enforcement agencies on both sides of the border. It should be noted that the agencies now participating in PNS and IBETs were similarly engaged prior to the inception of either initiative. A significant impact attributed to both initiatives is the improvement in the same relationships, intelligence, and resource sharing as well as the collaboration and cooperation across the law enforcement spectrum brought about by PNS and IBETs.

To be specific, PNS is a successful forum for strategic collaboration by participating agencies that share concerns regarding border security matters. PNS serves an important coordinating and liaison function for the myriad number of agencies engaged, Canadian and American, with border security or related investigative matters. While PNS is not an operational group, its most important and critical function is to provide a forum for collaboration amongst the agencies and then present these matters of concern to the appropriate components in Ottawa and Washington, D.C. For example, PNS has been working on matters concerning the inter-operability of communication amongst the various Canadian and U.S. law enforcement agencies working on the northern border. PNS is seeking solutions that will permit U.S. Border Patrol (USBP) agents to communicate directly with Royal Canadian Mounted Police (RCMP) members working joint enforcement operations. Secondly, PNS is seeking a legal solution to problems that arise when U.S. authorities are engaged in the pursuit of smugglers or illegal aliens who attempt to evade capture by fleeing into Canada. The same holds true for RCMP members who engage subjects who attempt to escape by fleeing into the United States. Moreover, in cases wherein a USBP agent is in need of immediate assistance in a life threatening situation in the United States and the nearest law enforcement officer was an RCMP member, the RCMP member would violate U.S. law by crossing the border to assist the agent. The converse holds true were a USBP agent to assist a RCMP member in Canada. PNS is seeking legal remedies for these matters.

The PNS operates at optimal efficiency and effectiveness in its coordination, liaison, and referral function; however, increased participation in PNS Conferences by local and county law enforcement agencies along the border is needed. Most of the municipal and county agencies operating on the northern frontier are rather small and lack funding that precludes significant travel outside their areas of responsibility. PNS presently has insufficient funding to underwrite the travel costs by those agencies to ensure their attendance. The amount of additional funding required is not known by DEA and is a matter for the PNS coordinating quad chair committee. The leadership for PNS in each jurisdiction is a committee of four, thus, the designation quad-chair committee.

The IBETs proved successful along the northern New York region in coordinating border security and interdiction efforts among the various agencies. The New York Division of the Drug Enforcement Administration (DEA) participates in operations conducted by the IBET at Cornwall, Canada, as well as the IBET in the Buffalo region. Specifically, DEA agents are pre-positioned and forward deployed to respond to the interdiction and seizure of illicit controlled substances that arise from IBET operations and to further those seizures by conducting appropriate investigations to fully identify, prosecute, and dismantle the drug trafficking organizations (DTOs) involved.

The IBETs have enhanced the coordination between the various U.S. law enforcement agencies on the border, particularly the USBP, and Canadian agencies. For example, prior to the inception of the IBETs, oftentimes a USBP vessel would be on patrol but no complementary Canadian vessel was in the region. Thus, when a USBP vessel engaged a suspect vessel that fled toward Canada, it was impossible to interdict the vessel as no Canadian resources were available. Today, as a direct result of the IBETs, the USBP and Canadian authorities coordinate their maritime patrols which substantially increases the likelihood of capture or thwarting the drug operation by forcing the smugglers to jettison the shipment. Previously, smugglers could evade capture and preserve their illicit shipment by returning to their native country and attempt the venture at a later date. The improved coordination and sharing of resources, information, and intelligence brought about by and from the collaboration of the participating IBET agencies has dramatically improved interdiction operations and efforts in the northern New York region.

The following is a representative sample of statistical seizures from the Cornwall IBET for calendar years 2002 and 2003 (combined):

Total Currency Seized:	$1.55 million
Total Value of Conveyances/Untaxed Cigarettes Seized:	$1, 209, 770
Total Drug Seizures by Weight:	1,877.96 pounds

The IBETs may be improved by future collocation and sufficient communication equipment and information systems to support IBET interdiction operations. At present, the DEA presence along the New York border with Canada is served by a Post of Duty at Plattsburgh staffed by three DEA Special Agents (SAs). Two of the SAs are located in the Plattsburgh region while the third is forward deployed to Massena, New York and works from the New York State Police (NYSP) barracks in Massena. In order to be able to respond to the growing trans-border threat posed by Canadian produced hydroponically grown marijuana, heroin, cocaine and precursor chemicals used in the manufacture of methamphetamine, DEA continually reevaluates its resource needs in the region to exploit investigative opportunities developed by IBETS.

The Bureau of Immigration and Customs Enforcement (BICE) has increased and continues to add SA personnel to Massena as well as Rouses Point, New York. The interdiction at the ports of entry (POEs) resulting from the enhanced BICE presence will present additional challenges for DEA which must be prepared to exploit those investigative opportunities as they arise.

Other enhancements for IBETs that would be helpful to law enforcement would include an amendment to Rule 6e of the Federal Rules of Criminal Procedure to allow U.S. agents to share information developed by U.S. Federal Grand Juries with Canadian authorities in connection with collaborative investigations. Additionally, it is suggested that both the U.S. and Canadian government modify existing law to grant U.S. and Canadian agents and officers limited law enforcement authority in the neighboring country to conduct pursuits, surveillance, and emergency requests for aid.

2. The Canadian government has now proposed the partial legalization or "decriminalization" of at least the possession of marijuana. We have several questions with respect to this development:

a. First, what impact do you believe this will have on patterns of drug smuggling? Will it increase the supply of the drug in Canada? Do you believe it will make it easier to grow, store and distribute the drug in Canada? Will it make it easier to smuggle the drug into the United States?

The prevailing view among the U.S. federal law enforcement community, as well as prosecuting attorneys, is that the immediate effect of the decriminalization of marijuana in small quantities in Canada will stimulate experimentation among young adults in the United States living within a reasonable driving distance of Canada. Thus, young adults or teens who would have been otherwise discouraged and not likely to experiment with marijuana fearing criminal prosecution in both the United States or Canada may travel to Canada to obtain and experiment with marijuana. It then follows that a certain proportion of those who experimented may become regular users. This will stimulate demand on both the Canadian as well as the United States side of the border, which will have a complementary effect on supply. Certain trends can be expected based upon previous experiences with respect to underage alcohol consumption by U.S. teens, who routinely travel to Canadian establishments willing to serve them alcohol. If Canada were to decriminalize marijuana, Canadian sources for hydroponically grown marijuana would likely proliferate. For example, the Toronto Municipal Police already estimate that more than 10,000 illicit marijuana growing operations currently exist within their jurisdiction. The decriminalization of marijuana in Canada will most certainly stimulate that burgeoning industry and will result in an increased supply of high-quality hydroponically grown marijuana in close proximity to the United States border.

In addition, it is expected that organized crime elements already in existence in Canada, such as the Hells Angels, will exploit and capitalize on this situation by utilizing their existing drug distribution structure to meet increased demand for the product in the United States. Thus, the increased smuggling and distribution of high quality hydroponically produced marijuana from Canada will intensify.

The decriminalization of small quantities of marijuana in Canada will impact the ability of Canadian law enforcement authorities to respond to the expected proliferation of illicit growing operations. The stigma attached to marijuana consumption in Canada will be significantly reduced resulting in increased experimentation and regular use. Organized criminal syndicates will exploit the increased demand by controlling illicit growing operations in the region. Associated criminal activity by organized as well as independent elements will further tax Canadian law enforcement resources and will dilute other enforcement operations.

While the enhanced and continually improved border security apparatus in the United States will make it increasingly more difficult to successfully smuggle illicit substances into the United States, the expected increase in demand and supply resulting from decriminalization in Canada will also tax U.S. border security agencies focusing on counter-terrorism matters as illegal cross border smuggling of marijuana will be expected to increase.

b. If Canada adopts such changes to its laws, how will your agency respond? What steps will you take to counteract the effect it has on drug smuggling?

If Canada, in fact, does decriminalize marijuana, the DEA will continue to monitor the evolving situation and pay particular attention to trend analysis. Working with our federal as well as our state and local partners, DEA must be able to quickly react to any emerging trend brought about by the decriminalization of marijuana in Canada. For example, increased cross border smuggling of marijuana and the proliferation of organized criminal smuggling DTOs brought by the decriminalization in Canada would cause DEA to re-evaluate its resources in the area to determine if a reallocation of SA positions to the region is warranted. The same holds true for BICE and the USBP who also predict a deteriorating marijuana smuggling situation brought on by decriminalization in Canada. Those agencies would probably need to evaluate their resource needs to respond to the changing threats.

c. If Mexico adopted similar changes to its laws, would you take identical steps? If not, why is there a difference in approach on the Southern and Northern borders?

It is expected that any similar situation brought on by the decriminalization of marijuana by the Republic of Mexico would engender a similar response by U.S. law enforcement authorities to meet the emerging threat. In essence, the response by DEA would be the same in both regions and only mitigated by the force structure already in place along the Southwest Border.

3. There are a number of state parks in your area of responsibility that are right on the border with Canada. What is the extent of drug smuggling, illegal immigration and other cross-border crime on state parks? What kind of operations does your agency have on state parks?

What is the state of cooperation between the state law enforcement personnel stationed at those parks and your agency?

Neither the DEA New York Division nor the USBP at Swanton, Vermont or Buffalo, New York sections have detected any emerging trend or have specific intelligence or evidence to suggest state parks are either more nor less likely to be used to smuggle illicit substances or aliens. It should be noted that the New York State Park Police have concentrated patrols within the state parks which are augmented by the NYSP, USBP, and the U.S. Coast Guard, where applicable. Thus, state parks are more likely to have an enhanced law enforcement presence as opposed to adjacent private or commercial property. The criminal DTOs and independent traffickers are more apt to use a border segment that is less often patrolled than the state parks.

The DEA along with the NYSP, USBP, and New York State Park Police (NYSPP) work in conjunction when investigative intelligence or information suggests a criminal element may use a state park for illegal purposes. The working relationship between DEA and the NYSP is superlative in every respect. DEA has an agent co-located with the NYSP at Massena and the two SAs in Plattsburgh work virtually all drug investigations jointly with the NYSP. In addition, the DEA enjoys a similar relationship with the NYSPP and the USBP across the region.

4. The Cattaraugus Indian Reservation occupies a stretch of the coastline on Lake Erie. What operations do you carry out to protect that coastline, and what, if any, kinds of smuggling are taking place there? What is the level of cooperation between your agency and tribal law enforcement agencies? Do you have operations in any other Indian reservations in the Buffalo area? How does this compare to the operations carried out by federal agencies at the Akwesasne (Mohawk) reservation along the St. Lawrence River in eastern New York?

DEA conducts no interdiction operations in the Cattaragus region, but is responsive to investigative intelligence or information.

Thus, DEA will initiate, coordinate and or assist other agencies based on actionable information or intelligence concerning drug trafficking at the border. In particular, that portion of the Cattaraugus Reservation along Lake Erie is primarily patrolled by maritime elements of the Erie County and Chautauqua County Sheriff's Offices which is augmented by the USBP and its aviation unit in the area.

A review of information, intelligence and previous investigations revealed no trend or evidence that the Cattaraugus Reservation was or is used to facilitate illicit drug smuggling. Anecdotal historical evidence indicated illicit liquor smuggling occurred on the reservation in years past and intelligence suggests the illicit smuggling of untaxed cigarettes occurs in the area today.

The DEA engages the Cattaraugus and Seneca Tribal Police when DEA enforcement operations occur in their areas of responsibility. The DEA Resident Office at Buffalo does not conduct operations on any reservation unless they involve an active criminal investigation. When active investigations involve the reservations, the DEA Buffalo Resident Office will engage the tribal police authorities at the appropriate stage of the investigation.

The same application of DEA investigative resources holds true for matters involving the Akwasasne Reservation. It should be noted that the NYSP are responsible for enforcing state law on the Akwasasne Reservation as the tribal police are currently without police authority in the State of New York. [Note: By a previous act of Congress, the responsibility and authority for policing the Akwasasne was delegated to the State of New York.] The DEA SAs assigned to the Plattsburgh Post of Duty work in conjunction with NYSP investigators on all criminal matters that may involve the Akwasasne Reservation. Of particular note, the Akwasasne Reservation was the site of significant civil unrest in years past and the NYSP is sensitive to any matter that may incite future unrest. Thus, DEA operations on the Akwasasne are conducted in close cooperation with the NYSP.

5. Recently the Canadian government adopted regulations to establish some control over the sale of methamphetamine precursor chemicals, such as the cold medicine pseudoephedrine. The regulations, as we understand them, essentially require the reporting of sales. Do you believe these regulations will be effective in reducing the amount of precursor chemicals smuggled into the United States? What additional measures do you believe Canada should take to control these chemicals?

The enhanced regulations enacted by the Canadian government will assist U.S. law enforcement agencies in tracking precursor chemicals involved in U.S. investigations. In addition, the new Canadian regulations will improve Canadian oversight with respect to the manufacture, sale, distribution, importation and exportation of precursor chemicals. As a result, we expect the diversion of licit chemicals into the flow of illicit trafficking in Canada to be reduced. Therefore, this reduction will have a complementary effect in the United States by eventually reducing the supply of precursor chemicals illegally smuggled into the United States.

At present, talks and negotiations between the Canadian government and the United States are ongoing with respect to this issue. It is expected that the Canadian government will review existing U.S. law and regulation of this industry and adopt appropriate measures as they see fit.

NORTHERN BORDER FIELD HEARING
May 19, 2003

Follow-up question from Chairman Dave Camp for the Record

Drug Enforcement Administration (DEA)

1. Are there any concerns about continued cooperation, especially with the Integrated Border Enforcement Teams (IBET), should legislation reforming criminal penalties for cannabis use become law in Canada?

We expect no change in the level of cooperation and collaboration on the part of Canadian law enforcement authorities if Canada decriminalizes the possession of small quantities of marijuana. The coordination and sharing of resources, information and intelligence resulting from IBET operations in concert with the Canadian authorities is expected to continue unabated. Moreover, the continuing threat of terrorism, as well as the threat posed by organized criminal syndicates and DTOs involved in the illicit distribution and smuggling of heroin, cocaine and synthetic drugs, will form the basis for continuing collaboration and cooperation with Canadian authorities even if significant decriminalization of marijuana in Canada were to occur.

Responses to Questions Posed by Representative John Shadegg (R-AZ) before the oversight hearing: Improving Security and Facilitating Commerce at the Northern Border: Field Hearings in Niagara Falls, New York.

1. What government entity is responsible for restoring law enforcement powers to the Tribal Police at the Akwasasne/St. Regis Mohawk Indian Reservation in Franklin County?

Response: Pursuant to an Act of Congress passed in 1948, 25 USC 232, which confers upon the State of New York jurisdiction over "offenses committed by or against Indians on Indian Reservations within the State of New York to the same extent as the courts of the State have jurisdiction over offenses committed elsewhere within the State as defined by the laws of the State……." the United States conferred responsibility for the Akwasasne/St. Regis Mohawk Reservation to the State of New York. Since the enactment of the above captioned law, the State of New York has been responsible for policing the reservation. Thus, the authority to confer law enforcement powers upon the Akwasasne Tribal Police rests with the Legislature and Governor of the State of New York.

2. Is there a burden imposed on the Tribal Police to handle drug trafficking?

Response: The Akwasasne Reservation, not unlike other Native American Reservations, is unique and culturally distinct from the surrounding community and region. To complicate matters, the reservation occupies territory in Canada as well as the United States; however, there is no controlled border crossing within the reservation. Therefore, the Tribal Police are uniquely positioned to monitor and control legal as well as illegal border traffic. In an effort to control illicit smuggling of narcotics and other licit merchandise, U.S. law enforcement authorities must rely upon the Tribal Police. They possess the ability to detect, identify, and interrupt illicit smuggling on and through the reservation and are the first bastion of defense. The Tribal Police are also the best and most reliable source of actionable intelligence concerning illegal activity within their area of responsibility. Thus, a significant burden is placed upon them to augment and assist other state and federal agencies charged with investigating and disrupting narcotics trafficking.

3. Regarding the exploitation of local residents in these remote locations by smugglers; come in and simply bribe them to help get drugs or people across the border……..I would appreciate if you would look into that issue as well and get back to me.

Response: Although there is no definitive evidence to support the following, it is our assumption based on training and expertise, that traffickers will exploit strategic as well as operational shortcomings of law enforcement and the law to benefit their illicit activities. Therefore, we must conclude that traffickers operating in, on and about the Akwasasne Reservation are aware the Tribal Police have no legal authority to investigate violations of state or federal law. Our assumption further concludes traffickers will exploit this weakness and focus illegal activities in areas where law enforcement is legally restricted, such as the Akwasasne Reservation.

Information and intelligence developed from investigations that involved the Akwasasne Reservation as well as the Adirondack region indicate smugglers of both illicit drugs and other commodities (liquor and or untaxed tobacco products and illegal aliens) utilize the Akwasasne Reservation and its residents to facilitate their illegal activities. For example, smugglers working in conjunction with both traditional as well as non-traditional organized crime elements have been able to recruit new members into their illegal organizations from the reservation and surrounding communities.

The social and economic ills that effect the region exacerbates the situation by making illegal smuggling more attractive, and therefore it is easier for smugglers to entice residents from the reservation and the region to participate in their illegal organizations. The unique cultural nature of the reservation makes it extremely difficult for law enforcement to conduct discrete and covert operations or to penetrate smuggling operations using non-resident agents or informants.

The geographic nature of the reservation permits uncontrolled access to either country through the reservation. Conversely, the unique cultural nature of the community also serves to enhance law enforcement since suspicious or clearly illegal activity by non-residents is readily discerned and reported quickly by the overwhelmingly law abiding citizenry who live on the reservation. At the same time, those who live on the reservation and who are involved in illegal smuggling can use their relationships with the law abiding residents in their community to further obfuscate their involvement in illegal activity.

U.S. CUSTOMS AND BORDER PROTECTION
Department of Homeland Security

1300 Pennsylvania Avenue, N.W., Washington, D.C. 20229

JUL 15 2003

The Honorable Mark E. Souder
Chairman
Committee on Government Reform
Subcommittee on Criminal Justice,
Drug Policy and Human Resources
U.S. House of Representatives
Washington, D.C. 20515

Dear Chairman Souder:

Thank you for your letter of June 3, 2003, regarding additional written questions for the record from the Subcommittee's May 19, 2003 field hearing in Niagara Falls, New York. Enclosed are the written responses to these additional questions.

I appreciate your interest in the Bureau of Customs and Border Protection. If we may offer further assistance, please contact me at (202) 927-1760.

Yours truly,

Richard F Quinn
Acting Assistant Commissioner
Office of Congressional Affairs

Enclosures

Vigilance ★ *Service* ★ *Integrity*

**COMMITTEE ON GOVERNMENT REFORM
SUBCOMMITTEE ON CRIMINAL JUSTICE, DRUG POLICY AND HUMAN RESOURCES**

**SELECT COMMITTEE ON HOMELAND SECURITY
SUBCOMMITTEE ON INFRASTRUCTURE AND BORDER SECURITY**

"IMPROVING SECURITY AND FACILITATING COMMERCE AT THE NORTHERN BORDER: FIELD HEARING IN NIAGARA FALLS, NEW YORK"

MAY 19, 2003

FOLLOW-UP QUESTIONS FOR THE RECORD FOR BUREAU OF CUSTOMS AND BORDER PROTECTION FROM CHAIRMAN MARK E. SOUDER

1. **What has been the specific impact of U.S.-Canadian cross-border law enforcement ventures such as Project Northstar and the IBET teams? What concrete results have they had? Could these initiatives be improved?**

Immigration and Customs Enforcement:

The Integrated Border Enforcement Teams (IBETs) have had a significant impact in improving law enforcement operations along the shared U.S/Canadian border. The IBETs have been directly responsible for an increased level of communication and coordination between U.S. and Canadian law enforcement officers. IBET operational activity effectively removes the "border advantage" from cross-border criminals.

The IBET concept started as a cooperative effort among the U.S. Customs service, U.S. Border patrol and the RCMP in 1994 in the state of Washington as a grassroots effort to combat the dramatic rise in the amount of hydroponically grown marijuana being smuggled into the United States. This innovative cross border task force was the first of its kind. The idea of multidisciplinary teams working in an integrated land, air and sea environment had never been tried before. Enhancing border integrity and security by investigating organizations and persons that pose a threat to national security or are involved in organized crime became a national priority.

Project Northstar's impact in the Pacific consists of bringing together agencies working on cross-border crime issues. Though Northstar is a non-operational entity, its successes are measured through facilitation of joint ventures, training and identifying common law enforcement obstacles. Northstar seeks solutions to problems through technology groups and bi-national governmental committees such as the Cross-Border Crime Forum.

Cross border weapons carriage, cross designation of foreign law enforcement officers, intelligence and communication working groups and legislation to allow foreign law enforcement officers to enter "between the ports of entry" are ongoing issues which are being addressed. With these IBET initiatives we will continue to improve our international enforcement efforts.

Another secondary IBET issue is that DEA is not a participating agency. The DEA/RCMP Memorandum of Understanding (MOU) has limited the efficiency of intelligence sharing within the IBET's, as the RCMP is required to give all drug intelligence to DEA per their MOU.

Customs and Border Protection:

The specific impact of U.S.-Canadian cross border law enforcement ventures such as Project North Star and IBET has produced excellent results. These ventures have resulted in frequent gatherings of international law enforcement entities that are able to address all the important issues that affect the international border and communities. The impact of these ventures allows both the U.S. and Canadian authorities to immediately address important law enforcement issues that affect the border such as Terrorist activity, alien smuggling, contraband smuggling and many other issues closely related.

IBET and Project North Star meetings have created a forum that allows all law enforcement agencies, Customs & Border Protection, Royal Canadian Mounted Police, New York State Police, Ontario Provincial Police, U.S. Coast Guard, Canada Customs and Revenue, Canada Immigration and Passport, and other important agencies to meet on a frequent basis as well as daily contact through telephone calls to share information, plan operations and pool resources to address any potential law enforcement situation. In many regions along our Northern border, including the area in question, law enforcement agencies from both countries are studying the feasibility of collocating intelligence assets to enhance information sharing capabilities and enforcement operations along our common border. Some areas such as Blaine, Washington have already done so.

Through these ventures, we have identified a major alien smuggling group and identified major organizers or leaders of the group. Over the past couple of months, the Border Patrol has arrested 5 members of this group in the act of smuggling. Pressure from the Niagara Frontier IBET has forced this Organization to move their smuggling operations west to Windsor/Detroit.

Niagara Frontier IBET has identified and continues to monitor a group of Middle Easterners that are involved in the smuggling of contraband (cigarettes, alcohol, etc.) which proceeds are believed to be sent over seas to organizations possibly supporting terrorist activities.

In 2001, U.S. Attorney General Ashcroft and former Solicitor General MacAuley signed a Joint Statement on Cooperation on Border Security and Regional Migration Issues. The number two- (2) item of this agreement was to "reinvigorate Project North Star". Along with this, item 24 of the Smart Border Action Plan stipulated that "joint bi-national priorities be established through Project North Star".

Since then, Project North Star has firmly established 5 Regional Coordination Groups across the United States and Canada. Each RCG is staffed by a quad chair representative, consisting of a U.S. and Canadian Federal representative and a U.S. and Canadian State Provincial and Local representative.

These groups have held numerous training conferences that have identified issues, which impact upon law enforcement activities. The two most significant issues are the cross border carrying of firearms by law enforcement personnel and the communications interoperability of law enforcement personnel. These two issues have been given to the Cross-Border Crime Forum, who has convened working groups Canadian) and (US to solve these problems. *Other issues have risen such as the revisiting of outdated cross border Memorandums of Understanding (MOUs) that hamper investigations and the need to standardize security clearances in order to share information more readily.*

Project North Star continues to convene meetings for the express purpose of sharing "best practices" and to learn how U.S. and Canadian law enforcement can better perform their duties. Improvements can be made by providing a more substantial budget in order to fund state and local agencies that are currently unable to attend these conferences due to small agency budgets. The present Project North Star budget is provided solely by the U.S. Border Patrol and is limited to funding conference locations and a select few people to travel to the conferences.

Presently the US Border Patrol provides three (3) full time positions to Project North Star under the direct supervision of the Chief Patrol Agent, Buffalo Sector. The Canadian government is studying the feasibility of placing a person at the Project North Star Coordination Center and a representative from the New York National Guard may be assigned there as well. A representative from a State Police, Sheriff Department or local Police Department should also be present in order to properly represent this portion of Project North Star. This position could be funded by the federal government much like it is done for local participation in a federal task force environment.

2. **The Canadian government has now proposed the partial legalization or "decriminalization" of the possession of marijuana. We have several questions with respect to this development:**

   A. **First, what impact do you believe this will have on patterns of drug smuggling? Will it increase the supply of the drug in Canada? Do you believe it will make it easier to grow, store, and distribute the drug in Canada? Will it make it easier to smuggle the drug into the United States?**

<u>Immigration and Customs Enforcement</u>:

A. The northern border will continue to feel the growing impact of drug smuggling as the distance between our respective countries laws grow further apart. A lax response to cannabis possession and cultivation will likely lead to more production and smuggling.

According to the Canadian Controlled Drugs and Substances Act, Marijuana Medical Access Regulations passed on June 4, 2001, individuals who receive the appropriate license and meet the specified requirements may be able to produce marijuana for their own personal/medical use. This certainly would increase the "legal" supply of the drug in Canada. As a corollary, it will make it easier to grow and store the drug for "legitimate" users. i.e. medical users. A potential consequence of this "legal" supply is the diversion of marijuana production to individuals who do not have the proper authority to possess the drug. Canada may also see a cottage industry of false documentation begin to grow as individuals who want to produce the drug without the proper permit and license may look to these underground sources for false identities and permits. We do not however believe that the smuggling of the drug into the United States would be made any easier simply because of its decriminalization in Canada. Possession of marijuana would still be illegal in the United States.

<u>Customs and Border Protection:</u>

A. The proposed partial legalization or "decriminalization" of the possession of marijuana in Canada would likely create a larger, more accessible, and cheaper supply of the drug in Canada. It would be logical to assume that some consumers in the United States would travel to Canada to take advantage of this cheaper and more accessible market. Consequently, one might expect an increase in smuggling activities associated with passenger vehicles. Also, if this situation makes marijuana more accessible in commercial quantities, but it is highly regulated and taxed by Canada, there would be a motivation to increase profits by smuggling it to the U.S. market.

B. If Canada adopts such changes to its laws, ho will your agencies respond? What steps will you take to counteract the effect it has on drug smuggling?

Immigration and Customs Enforcement:

B. Our northern border offices would remain vigilant for increased personal use traffic entering through our ports of entry. The quantity of marijuana detected crossing the northern border increases every year. The Cannabis reform legislation will likely have little effect on this trend, already at a critical level. A move towards decriminalization indicates the smuggling problem will be with us for some time to come, formally indemnifying the abusers of the drug from criminal sanctions. We will continue with our efforts to disrupt the supply of the drug through interdiction and eliminate as much of the responsible organization as possible through joint investigative strategies with law enforcement agencies on both sides of the border.

Attacking drug related money laundering is also essential to impact the cross-border bi-directional smuggling. The incentive to smuggle is profit and those profits continue to move across the border in bulk.

Customs and Border Protection:

Should Canada adopt this proposal, the Bureau of Customs and Border Protection (BCBP) would increase its vigilance concerning drug smuggling and direct examination resources along the Northern Border in correlation with any trends in seizures. If seizures of marijuana secreted in passengers' vehicles increase, the number of secondary inspections will increase. This activity will place a strain on secondary inspection capacity and could increase infrastructure costs in terms of additional secondary inspection facilities.

C. If Mexico adopted similar changes to its laws, would you take identical steps? If not, why is there a difference in approach on the Southern and Northern borders?

Immigration and Customs Enforcement:

C. The southern border has historically been a major transit zone for the smuggling of bulk quantities of marijuana into the United States. The smuggling threat posed by the U.S.-Mexican border is substantially different than the northern border threat. Similar changes in Mexican law to decriminalize marijuana would not change our southern border anti-smuggling strategies.

Customs and Border Protection:

C. If Mexico adopts similar changes; BCBP would also increase its vigilance concerning drug smuggling along the Southern Border and direct examination resources in correlation with any trends in seizures.

3. There are a number of state parks in your areas of responsibility that are right on the border with Canada. What is the extent of drug smuggling, illegal immigration and other cross-border crime on state parks? What is the state of cooperation between the state law enforcement personnel stationed at those parks and your federal agencies?

Customs and Border Protection:

There are approximately 33 New York State Parks located within our area of responsibility that are adjacent to the border. Officers of the New York State Parks Police Department frequently patrol these parks. Through our IBETs we are in frequent contact with Offices of the NYS Parks Police. They are an important part of the Intelligence network established in New York State. Many of the parks have park managers or caretakers, who report any suspicious activity to the Police or U.S. Border immediately upon witnessing and such activity.

4. The Cattaraugus Indian Reservation occupies a stretch of coastline on Lake Erie. What operations do you carry out to protect the coastline, and what, if any smuggling are taking place there? What is the level of cooperation between your agencies and tribal law enforcement agencies? Do you have any operations in any other Indian Reservations in this area? Hoe does this compare to the operations carried out by the Border Patrol and other federal agencies at the Akwesasne (Mohawk) Reservation along the St. Lawrence River in eastern New York?

Immigration and Customs Enforcement:

It is difficult to compare and contrast enforcement operations that occur on the Indian reservations that are located in the upstate New York area. The Cattaraugus Indian Reservation is separated from Canada by Lake Erie (20 miles) while the Akwesasne Reservation is separated by the St. Lawerence River (1-Mile). Additionally the area directly across the river from the Akwasasne is also a Canadian Indian Reservation. As such, the geography along the St Lawrence provides smugglers direct smuggling routes.

BICE maintains a lead in investigations concerning smuggled/counterfeit cigarettes that were destined to the Cattaraugus Indian Reservation. BICE coordinates their enforcement activity with the New York State Police before executing search or arrest warrants on the Cattaraugus Indian Reservation. Recently, BICE successfully conducted search warrants on the Cattaraugus

Indian Reservation utilizing law enforcement personnel from the NY State Police, Sheriffs Department, Border Patrol, ATF and New York State Taxation.

With regards to the Akwasasne Indian Reservation, BICE is continually investigating criminal organizations that smuggle marijuana and currency through the reservation's lands. BICE has developed an excellent working relationship with the Tribal Police on the Akwesasne Indian Reservation. Additionally, BICE has established a joint task force in Massena, New York consisting of the local police, sheriff's department, New York State Police and on occasion, agents from DEA. Utilizing the Massena IBET we have conducted successful anti-smuggling operations along the Akwesasne Indian Reservation.

The law enforcement cooperation between the state law enforcement personnel within the area of responsibility for BICE/Buffalo is outstanding. The federal state and local agencies work well together.

Customs and Border Protection:

The Cattaraugus Indian Reservation occupies a stretch of the coastline on Lake Erie. This Cattaraugus Reservation is unlike the St. Regis Mohawk (Akwesasne) Reservation in that the Akwesasne saddles both sides of the international border stretching across the St. Lawrence River. The Cattaraugus is located on the Lake Erie coastline, with a distance of approximately 14 miles across from the U.S. to Canada. The Reservation is patrolled by Tribal Police from the Seneca Nation's Marshal Department, who provide all law enforcement agencies with cell phone numbers for contact with them 24 hours a day. Cooperation with Tribal Police has greatly improved since Sept. 11, 2001, through improved communication and cooperation. Support from the Marshal's office has been excellent on both the Cattaraugus Reservation and the Allegany Reservation.

Off-Reservation law enforcement agencies continually patrol the reservation boundaries. Cattaraugus County Sheriff's Dept. and New York State Police units are forever vigilant in this regard. Smuggling activity at this location is not an issue at this time due to the concentration of law enforcement agencies in a combined effort, compared to the Akwesasne Reservation, where smuggling of people and narcotics is very prevalent. Enforcement of activity associated with the Awkesasne is a much more difficult issue then at Cattaraugus and Allegany Reservations.

5. Recently the Canadian government adopted regulations to establish some control over the sale of methamphetamine precursor chemicals, such as the cold medicine pseudoephederine. The regulations, as we understand them, essentially require the reporting of sales. Do you believe these regulations will be effective in reducing the amount of precursor

chemicals smuggled into the United States? What additional measures do you believe Canada should take to control these chemicals?

Immigration and Customs Enforcement:

The Canadian Precursor Control Regulations (effective January 2003), which are part of the Canadian Controlled Drugs and Substances Act passed in 1997, allow for the control of precursors by regulating for their import, export, production and distribution in Canada. There are a number of measures that control precursor chemicals in Canada. Other important measures which are included in the law require licensed dealers to take precautions to insure the safety and security of the precursors at the site and during transportation; record keeping to insure internal controls of the chemicals; reporting thefts or loss of the chemical, the chemical's destruction, end-use declarations and suspicious transaction reporting. We do believe that these regulations will have a positive impact in reducing the amount of precursors smuggled into the United States. BICE has already seen a drop in the number of U.S. CBP/BICE northern border pseudoephedrine seizures.

Since the enforcement of these news regulations and laws is still in its infancy the full ramifications of their effect have not yet been seen. Canada has initiated an "education/outreach" effort with Canadian precursor suppliers to contact the appropriate law enforcement agency when suspicious transactions are encountered. We should assist Canadian lawmakers in drafting legislation to establish permanent sentencing guidelines for drug offenses. We suggest that Health Canada and the RCMP work jointly to develop an infrastructure to conduct background investigations on precursor importers or exporters.

6. What percentage of trucks crossing the border in your area of responsibility are enrolled in the Free and Secure Trade (FAST) program?

Customs and Border Protection:

Nationally there are 254 FAST Highway Carriers and 3,500 FAST Commercial Drivers, 600 of which were enrolled in Buffalo. There are approximately 3,000 Customs Trade Partnership Against Terrorism (C-TPAT) Importers. The overall capacity for the Port of Buffalo is unlimited. All of our commercial truck lanes (7 total) are FAST equipped. As FAST enrollment grows we will be able to dedicate additional truck lanes to accommodate FAST processing. In May 2003, less than 1% of the total Border Cargo Selectivity (BCS) entries cleared as "FAST". To be considered "FAST" there must be merchandise from a C-TPAT shipper, transportation from a FAST highway carrier, being driven by a FAST commercial driver and entered/released by Pre-Arrival Processing System (PAPS) or the National Customs Automation Prototype (NCAP), which are both FAST approved release methods.

FAST STATS for Buffalo Field Office: 05/05/03 through 06/12/03			
Buffalo Service Port		**Champlain Service Port**	
Total Truck BCS entries	119,503	Total Truck BCS Entries	78,395
Entries with C-TPAT Importers	5,256	Entries with C-TPAT Importers	817
Entries with C-TPAT Importers+Fast Carrier (No FAST Driver)	749	Entries with C-TPAT Importers+Fast Carrier (No FAST Driver)	22
Entries with C-TPAT Importers+Fast Carrier+FAST Driver	102	Entries with C-TPAT Importers+Fast Carrier+FAST Driver	13

7. What steps have your agencies taken to protect the physical integrity of the bridges and other port of entry facilities and infrastructures from terrorist attack or other damage? What cooperative efforts have you undertaken with the local bridge and port authorities to enhance infrastructure security?

Customs and Border Protection:

BUFFALO: We have met with the Border Patrol, Coast Guard and State Police and have coordinated first and second rung infrastructure security sweeps on a recurring basis. We have met with both the Peace Bridge and Niagara Fall Bridge Authorities on numerous occasions and have cooperatively developed actions that increase security of our U.S. compounds as well as that of their infrastructure. These actions include:

- an increase in their private security forces made up of off duty police officers focused on challenging individuals on and near the bridges as well as restricting access to our facilities;
- coordinated parking security, building security, lighting and camera upgrades;
    - coordinated communication protocols and logistics for the bomb threat response teams;
    - coordinated rapid installation of Radiation Portal Monitors and 24x7 mobile VACIS footprints; and,
    - coordinated truck traffic, HAZMAT and Continuity of Operations Plan (COOP) communication protocols.

In addition, the following security measures have been taken at the other service ports:

ALEXANDRIA BAY: The port of Alexandria Bay has full time New York State Troopers assigned to the port to assist us in securing the port from possible terrorist attacks.

CHAMPLAIN: While land border locations in the Champlain and Trout River area are not covered by a bridge or port authority, other steps have been taken to mitigate this and protect POEs/stations from terrorist attack. These efforts include:

- ensuring that officers are vigilant and aware of their surroundings;
- restricting access to portions of our facilities;
- the installation of Customs Area Security Systems (CASC) and hardening of locations with gates and video surveillance technology;
- the use of non-intrusive inspection technology such as radiation portal monitors, radiation pagers, and VACIS to assist port personnel in identifying threats to the infrastructure; and,
- coordinating with the Federal Protective Service and the Border Patrol to provide a response capability or increased patrols. In addition, close relationships with New York State Police have added a response capability if necessary. This is especially important due to the absence of a bridge or port authority in the Champlain/Trout River area.

8. Some older studies of "fastpass" systems like SENTRI and NEXUS have suggested that the impact of these programs on wait times at the ports of entry have been limited-not only for those traveling in the general, non dedicated lanes, but even for those participating in the program. (See, e.g., *Inspection of the Secure Electronic Network for Travelers' Rapid Inspection,* U.S. Dept. of Justice Office of the Inspector General, Report No. I-2000-019, June 2000.) Have subsequent studies demonstrated that these programs are now producing significant results in terms of reduced wait times? What has been the experience at the ports of entry in your area of responsibility?

<u>**Customs and Border Protection:**</u>

The NEXUS and SENTRI programs were primarily established to allow known low-risk travelers a means to rapidly transit the border and the participation in these programs has grown significantly since the previous studies were conducted. These programs not only allow travelers a predictable wait time but they also permit the inspection services to focus their law enforcement efforts on the relatively unknown potentially higher-risk traffic.

Nationally, the NEXUS and SENTRI systems have enrolled over 100,000 travelers, which have made millions of entries into the United States. Only a handful of violations have been detected from this highly screened border crossing population. Travelers enrolled in the NEXUS and SENTRI systems are inspected in seconds, the majority in less than ten, and they typically transit the entire port area in a few minutes. Where fully implemented, NEXUS and SENTRI have had a significant impact on wait times. Ports in which NEXUS and SENTRI are fully operational report that 20% of their peak hour traffic enters the United States through the NEXUS or SENTRI lanes.

In Buffalo, the NEXUS lane located at the Peace Bridge POE became operational on January 30, 2003. The POE has not yet reached the heavy passenger traffic volumes that are experienced during the summer months and, as such, there have not been any significant wait times to see what impact that the NEXUS lane may have in wait time reduction. For the month of April 2003, there were 1,857 NEXUS cards used out of 195,806 vehicle crossings, less than 1% of the traffic. Until the enrollment for NEXUS has increased AND the heavy passenger vehicle traffic months have been observed, no determination can be made as to the potential for a positive impact on wait time reductions. The three Niagara Falls Bridges, Rainbow, Whirlpool and Lewiston, are scheduled to be on line by mid August 2003.

A "fastpass" program that addresses commercial wait time is the Free and Secure Trade (FAST) program, which is still in its infancy. Understandably, the impact on average wait time is minimal at present. FAST will have a positive impact on wait time once enrollment grows. Open enrollment began in January 2003 and enrollment numbers are growing steadily each month. Presently there are 5 FAST Driver Enrollment Centers (EC) and 6 additional EC's will be opened by December 2003. We believe the expansion of FAST across the northern border (and southern border) will greatly aid our enrollment efforts.

9. When Border Patrol agents apprehend persons engaged in illegal activity on the border in the Buffalo Sector, what resources do they have to identify those persons? Are they able to determine if those persons are wanted by any other federal or state law enforcement agency, and do they make that determination in each case? Please identify all relevant databases or other systems that Border Patrol agents in the Buffalo Sector are able to access, and state whether they are accessed in the case of each apprehended person?

<u>Customs and Border Protection:</u>

All apprehended individuals are identified through systems on both sides of the border. Border Patrol agents traditionally search many databases through our communications room with the assistance of Law Enforcement Communications Assistants – LECA's. While the LECA check subjects through the available databases, the subject's name and biographical data are forwarded to all members of the IBET - RCMP, New York State Police, Ontario Provincial Police, U.S. Customs, Niagara Regional Police, Canada Customs, Canada Immigration and the F.B.I. through the JTTF.

There are a variety of systems used to identify suspects well as an immediate fingerprinting and forwarding of prints to the FBI when subjects are to be held in custody. This check usually results in a response from the FBI fingerprint unit within a short period of time that is usually less than a couple of hours at most.

Buffalo Sector Border Patrol Agents have the following resources to identify apprehended persons engaged in illegal activity:

1. Local Apprehension File
2. IDENT (Automated fingerprint identification system
3. ENFORCE (Enforcement Case Tracking System)
4. NAILS (National Automated Immigration Lookout System)
5. CIS (Central Index System)
6. NIIS (Non-Immigrant Information System)
7. STSC (Student/School System)
8. CLAIMS (Computer Linked Application Information Management System)
9. TECS (Treasury Enforcement Communications System)
10. NCIC (National Crime Information Center)
11. DCJS (Division of Criminal Justice Service)
12. NYSPIN (New York State Police Information System). Automatically checks wants, local and Nationwide, NY parole, violent felony, database.
13. NLETS (National Law Enforcement Telecommunication System)
14. CPIC (Canadian Police Information Center)
15. CNI (Criminal Name Index) – Canada
16. NSEERS (National Security Entry-Exit Registration System)
17. FBI Data Base (Telephone check with local FBI office of their database's)
18. EPIC (El Paso Information Center)
19. I-68 Database (Canadian Border Boat Landing Program)
20. EOIR (Executive Office for Immigration Review)
21. DACS (Deportable Alien Control System)
22. ANSIR (Automated Nationwide System for Immigration Review)
23. SEVIS (Student and Exchange Visitor Program)
24. CIC (Canadian Immigration Center) Telephonically conduct landed immigrant status in Canada)
25. IBIS (Interagency Border Information System)

The Buffalo Sector Border Patrol Agents are readily able to ascertain if a particular subject is wanted locally, nationally, or in Canada. All aliens are checked for wants and warrants on a routine basis per Sector standard operating procedures.

The following database searches are conducted on all aliens:
1. Local Apprehension File
2. NAILS
3. TECS
4. CIS
5. NIIS
6. CLAIMS

7. STUDENT
8. NCIC/DCJS
9. IDENT/ENFORCE

HOUSE SELECT COMMITTEE ON HOMELAND SECURITY
SUBCOMMITTEE ON INFRASTRUCTURE AND BORDER SECURITY

"IMPROVING SECURITY AND FACILITATING COMMERCE AT THE NORTHERN BORDER: FIELD HEARING IN NIAGARA FALLS, NEW YORK"

MAY 19, 2003

FOLLOW-UP QUESTIONS FOR THE RECORD FOR BUREAU OF CUSTOMS AND BORDER PROTECTION FROM CHAIRMAN DAVE CAMP

1. **For the last 200 years, the primary mission of the Customs Service has been to collect revenue and to ensure that imports flow smoothly across the border. Today, Customs collects more than $20 billion in revenue each year. Even before its transfer into the Dept. of Homeland Security, Customs has taken on many security functions because of its unique border presence. What disruptions to legitimate travel and commerce you have witnessed since September 11th and what can be done to mitigate similar problems from happening in the future?**

Customs and Border Protection:

BUFFALO: Since the initial delays immediately after 9/11 we have had very limited disruptions to legitimate travel and commerce. The increase in the staff of Bureau of Customs and Border Protection (BCBP) Inspectors as well as Automated Targeting Systems (ATS), Radiation Portal Monitors (RPMs) and Vehicle and Container Inspection System (VACIS) machines have mitigated the impact of increased enforcement activity. Adding License Plate Readers (LPRs) as well as our continued efforts at streamlining legacy INS and Customs resources/operations will continue to mitigate future impact. As programs such as Free and Secure Trade (FAST) and NEXUS grow in number of participants, we will further be able to concentrate our enforcement efforts on the truly high-risk shipments and travelers and further facilitate legitimate trade and travel.

ALEXANDRIA BAY: Processing of traffic, both commercial and private, just after 9/11 was slowed to a crawl as BCBP began to look much closer at identification and cargo. As time has progressed Inspectors have become better at looking more deeply into commercial loads and doing trunk and hood inspections.

Alexandria Bay has been funded to build a third commercial lane, which will allow for faster processing of commercial trucks. Massena now has a VACIS that allows for faster processing of commercial vehicles. Ogdensburg will be receiving a VACIS in mid July, which will provide for faster examination capabilities and will also decrease wait times.

CHAMPLAIN: Added staffing and the deployment of new non-intrusive inspection technology has allowed us to facilitate the movement of legitimate trade and travelers while at the same time allowing us to focus on higher risk cargo. Additionally, the implementation of programs such as NEXUS, FAST, and Customs Trade Partnership Against Terrorism (C-TPAT), which use a risk management approach, will allow us to facilitate the movement of legitimate trade and travelers.

2. How quickly and effectively can interoperable computer systems and the submission of electronic manifests from shippers prior to arrival be implemented? How can these technologies be brought online while keeping borders open to legitimate cross-border travel and commerce moving?

<u>Customs and Border Protection:</u>

Electronic manifest data is already being received in advance of conveyance arrival for cargoes being imported by ocean, rail and air carriers. If trucks are carried into the US via rail, the manifest data is transmitted electronically by the importing railroads. The acquisition of advance manifest data on direct truck arrivals is being addressed under the CBP development initiative known as the Automated Commercial Environment (ACE) that will bring the direct arrival trucks into the electronic reporting environment in calendar 2004.

- Ocean, rail and air cargo manifests are already being received in electronic format from the transportation partners in advance of arrival at the land, coastwise and air corridor ports of entry. Plans are well underway to enfranchise direct arrival truck traffic into the electronic manifest environment during 2004 via the CBP "ACE" initiative and overall automated development is fully aligned with the objectives and milestones of the Trade Act of 2002.

- CBP is in the process of co-locating Immigration Inspectors and Customs Inspectors within the Primary Inspections facilities of the top 70 airports 12/31/03. This system and application access will be accomplished via a shared network.

- Co-location of secondary inspection facilities for legacy Customs, Immigration and Agriculture inspectors is also underway.

- CBP and ICE currently share access to each other's intranet and web portal sites, which provides access to each legacy agency's (Customs and INS) applications.

Through the use of existing automated applications such as the Automated Manifest System (AMS) and the implementation of the new ACE manifest application for trucks, CBP will deploy an array of robust electronic applications

that will evaluate shipment risk before arrival and reinforced on the ground with powerful non-intrusive inspection technologies (NII), such as high energy gamma and x-ray devices, CBP field forces will screen and examine cargo with intelligence and technology before goods enter the US. Equipped with the aforementioned tools and staffed with a fully integrated field force constituted from the legacy Customs, Immigration and Agriculture positions, CBP will be able to keep our borders open to legitimate cross-border travel and international commerce while protecting the people, economy and agriculture of the United States.
Beginning in 2004, Release 4 of the Automated Commercial Environment (ACE) will enable more efficient electronic manifest capabilities at the border. Initially these capabilities will be available for trucks at land border ports. In 2005, capabilities will be expanded as the electronic manifest becomes the standard for all modes of transportation. The electronic-Release system design incorporates all existing cargo release data in a single, consolidated view, eliminating the current burden on CBP officers to manually switch between different ACS release modules. e-Release will also capture in-bond processing, including moves to bonded warehouses and Foreign Trade Zones. Transponder and proximity card technologies, incorporated in this Release, will enable total electronic processing, eliminating the need for paper manifests and bar codes. By subsuming and consolidating existing release systems, ACE will broaden capabilities without interfering with existing release processes.

ACE Release 4 is currently planned to be deployed incrementally to 7 land border
ports, beginning in Spring/Summer 2004. Deployment will begin at one port followed by an evaluation period or pilot of approximately 6 weeks. A second port deployment and similar 6-week evaluation will follow. After the second pilot, deployments to the five additional ports will be accomplished over the subsequent 2-month period. Deployment beyond the initial 7 ports is still in the planning phase and is dependent of FY 04 funding.

3. How many passengers and cargo traffic pass through points of entry in the Buffalo Sector on an average day?

<u>Customs and Border Protection:</u>

	Buffalo Field Office[1]		
	FY 2001	FY 2002	FYTD 2003
Commercial Trucks	5,277	5,342	5,633
Passenger Vehicles	29,776	28,790	24,293

	Service Port of Buffalo		
	FY 2001	FY 2002	FYTD 2003
Commercial Trucks	3,130	3,228	3,226
Passenger Vehicles	20,997	19,990	16,774
	Service Port of Champlain		
	FY 2001	FY 2002	FYTD 2003
Commercial Trucks	1,055	1,016	1,005
Passenger Vehicles	2,799	2,807	2,129

[1] The Buffalo Field Office includes data for the entire Buffalo Sector, which includes the Buffalo and Champlain Service Ports and all the smaller ports of entry within the Buffalo Sector.

4. How many individual travelers have signed up with the NEXUS system? What is the maximum capacity of this system given the current infrastructure?

Customs and Border Protection:

BUFFALO: As of June 12, 2003, there were 7,500 NEXUS applications submitted with 5,290 NEXUS cards issued for the Buffalo-Niagara Falls area. Unlike FAST, NEXUS is currently site specific only and not a universal card that can be utilized at all NEXUS crossings in the country. There have been 43,967 NEXUS cards issued nationally as of May 30, 2003.

The temporary Buffalo-Niagara Falls NEXUS enrollment center has been able to process approximately 160 applicants per week, which would average 8,320 approved applicants per year. NEXUS cards are good for 5 years; thus, approximately 41,600 applicants could be processed before NEXUS cards began expiring and would be up for renewal. A new, permanent NEXUS enrollment center is scheduled to open in August, 2003, and the number of applicants that can be processed could be increased due to the elimination of the present physical constraints of the temporary enrollment center.

For the month of May 2003, there were 511,352 passenger vehicle crossings in the Port of Buffalo. If 41,600 NEXUS cards were issued, this would be 8% of the total traffic and would be easily handled by bridge infrastructure.

NATIONAL: As of June 1, 2003, there were 44,986 travelers enrolled in the NEXUS program.

- 33,794 in Blaine, WA (Peace Arch, Pacific Highway and Point Roberts)
- 6,235 in Detroit, MI (Port Huron, Ambassador Bridge, Windsor Tunnel)
- 4,957 in Buffalo, NY (Peace Bridge)—data from above is more recent

The maximum capacity of any given NEXUS site is dependent on the layout of the site, the number of lanes, and the traffic crossing patterns. For example, the NEXUS DCL at Peace Arch has a high capacity because it has a dedicated road that extends well back into Canada. Also, the traffic crossing at Peace Arch is evenly distributed over the day, with no single hour crossing more than 10% of the total day's traffic. On the other hand, the NEXUS lane at the Ambassador Bridge has a very short dedicated approach lane. NEXUS travelers mix with other traffic on the bridge and do not separate until the vehicles are off the bridge and on the approach apron. Also, 60% of the NEXUS traffic at the Ambassador Bridge crosses between 5 a.m. and 9 a.m., with the remaining 40% of traffic crossing between 9 a.m. and 8 p.m. Although the Ambassador Bridge lane has only been open since January 2003, planning has begun to open a second lane in order to alleviate the morning rush hour congestion.

5. How many people use the FAST system? What is the maximum capacity of this system given the current infrastructure?

Customs and Border Protection:

Nationally there are 254 FAST Highway Carriers and 3,500 FAST Commercial Drivers, 600 of which were enrolled in Buffalo. There are approximately 3,000 Customs Trade Partnership Against Terrorism (C-TPAT) Importers. The overall capacity for the Port of Buffalo is unlimited. All of our commercial truck lanes (7 total) are FAST equipped. As FAST enrollment grows we will be able to dedicate additional truck lanes to accommodate FAST processing. In May 2003, less than 1% of the total Border Cargo Selectivity (BCS) entries cleared as "FAST". To be considered "FAST" there must be merchandise from a C-TPAT shipper, transportation from a FAST highway carrier, being driven by a FAST commercial driver and entered/released by Pre-Arrival Processing System (PAPS) or the National Customs Automation Prototype (NCAP), which are both FAST approved release methods.

FAST STATS for Buffalo Field Office: 05/05/03 through 06/12/03			
Buffalo Service Port		**Champlain Service Port**	
Total Truck BCS entries	119,503	Total Truck BCS Entries	78,395

Entries with C-TPAT Importers	5,256	Entries with C-TPAT Importers	817
Entries with C-TPAT Importers+Fast Carrier (No FAST Driver)	749	Entries with C-TPAT Importers+Fast Carrier (No FAST Driver)	22
Entries with C-TPAT Importers+Fast Carrier+FAST Driver	102	Entries with C-TPAT Importers+Fast Carrier+FAST Driver	13

6. Has a Port Security Assessment been completed for the Port of Buffalo? If not, is one underway or planned in the future?

Customs and Border Protection:

Private consultants that the Bridge Commissions hired have performed security assessments.

7. With respect to facilitating the flow of traffic at border crossings, what are your views on providing pre-inspection sites further into the interior of the country versus expanding the infrastructure at the border?

Customs and Border Protection:

The goals of critical infrastructure protection and facilitation of legitimate trade can be accomplished through the "reverse inspection" and "shared facilities" concepts, discussed in the Shared Border Accord meetings with Canada. Currently, the Bureau of Customs and Border Protection (BCBP) has no legal authority to enforce U.S. laws in Canada, and as such, we cannot effectively accomplish our anti-terrorism, narcotics interdiction, and trade enforcement missions. However, BCBP has put great effort into developing a bilateral proposal with the Canadian government that would give BCBP enforcement authority in Canada, where appropriate. Efforts in this area are ongoing.

8. Are there any concerns about continued cooperation, especially with the Integrated Border Enforcement Teams (IBET), should legislation reforming criminal penalties for cannabis use become law in Canada?

Customs and Border Protection:

The decriminalization of small amounts of marijuana in a person's possession is problematic for Canadian law enforcement as it removes several options that they might be able to use in dealing with criminals. However, this decriminalization is for small amounts found on the person of someone in Canada, and should have minimal effect, if any on IBET cooperation. According to senior RCMP sources in Canada, the decriminalization does not remove the criminal codes for the importation, exportation, or smuggling, of marijuana.

Therefore, while law enforcement entities from both countries are watching the situation, law enforcement officers from both countries maintain similar focus on enforcement activities along our common border.

Immigration and Customs Enforcement:

The mission of the IBETs is to enhancing border integrity and security by investigating organizations and persons that pose a threat to national security or are involved in organized crime. Changes in Canadian law to decriminalize small amounts of marijuana would not have a significant impact on our IBET teams as we do not normally investigate cases that involve small amounts of narcotics. These cases are referred to state and local authorities for prosecution. IBETs work to disrupt and dismantle large-scale international criminal organizations.

Continued cooperation from our RCMP IBET partners in British Columbia, Canada looks to be long term with no plans to change course given the possible legislation reforms. IBET targets the smuggling of all commodities across the border and is not seen as a strictly marijuana smuggling initiative but rather a border integrity initiative.

U.S. CANADIAN CROSS-BORDER

QUESTION: What has been the specific impact of U.S.-Canadian cross-border law enforcement ventures such as Project Northstar and the IBET teams? What concrete results have they had? Could these initiatives be improved?

ANSWER: The Coast Guard experienced a positive impact, above and beyond normal operations, as the result of the U.S./Canadian cross border law enforcement ventures such as Project Northstar and the IBET teams. The U.S. Coast Guard, U.S. Bureau of Immigration and Customs Enforcement, U.S. Bureau of Customs and Border Protection, Citizenship and Immigration Canada, Royal Canadian Mounted Police, and Canada Customs and Revenue Agency are the core national agencies responsible for national oversight of IBETs. These initiatives tremendously assist the Coast Guard with intelligence, joint operations, tactics, information sharing and interagency cooperation. For example, since the IBET initiative began in the Ninth Coast Guard District, a 40 percent increase in overall seizures and arrests has been recorded. This includes law enforcement actions involving marijuana, cocaine, hashish, steroids, cigarettes; and illegal migrants. As these types of joint cross-border law enforcement activities mature, law enforcement effectiveness and border security will improve.

CANADIAN DECRIMINALIZATION

QUESTION: As you are probably aware, the Canadian government is considering the partial legalization or "decriminalization" of at least the possession of marijuana. We have several questions with respect to this development:

First, what impact do you believe this will have on patterns of drug smuggling? Will it increase the supply of the drug in Canada? Do you believe it will make it easier to grow, store and distribute the drug in Canada? Will it make it easier to smuggle the drug into the U.S.? If Canada adopts such changes to its laws, how will your agency respond? What steps will you take to counteract the effect it has on drug smuggling?

ANSWER: Although the impact on growing, storing, and distributing the drug in Canada will depend on the final shape of the Canadian legislation, the Coast Guard does not foresee any major changes in drug smuggling patterns as a result of the current version of the Cannabis Reform Bill (C-38). The Canadian law enforcement community, including the Canadian officials who are sponsoring this legislation, realize that many people will misinterpret the "decriminalization of marijuana" to mean that the use and possession of small amounts is legal and therefore without penalty of law. This is not the case and the production or transportation of any drug will still carry considerable penalties in Canada. Additionally, the new legislation, as currently drafted, increases penalties for commercial growers enhancing efforts to deter production and transportation.

Regardless of the results inside Canada, it will not be easier to smuggle into the United States because U.S. laws and enforcement efforts will not decrease or become more tolerant. The Coast Guard will continue to monitor this development and will base responses on a thorough analysis of emerging trends.

STATE PARK BORDERS

QUESTION: There are a number of state parks in your areas of responsibility that are right on the aquatic border with Canada. What is the extent of drug smuggling, illegal immigration and other cross-border crime into state parks? What kind of operations do you have on or near state parks? What is the state of cooperation between the state law enforcement personnel stationed at those parks and your personnel?

ANSWER: State parks are subject to state jurisdiction. The Coast Guard is a federal law enforcement agency and does not operate in exclusive state waters. However, under 14 USC 141 the Coast Guard may, when requested, assist state authorities in executing their responsibilities.

Additionally, the Coast Guard is part of the Smart Border Program. This program is a cooperative operation promoting multi-agency cooperation by addressing issues related to Ferry Terminals, Intelligent Transportation System, Critical Infrastructure Protection, Integrated Border Enforcement Teams, Joint Enforcement Coordination and Integrated Intelligence.

INDIAN RESERVATION BORDERS

QUESTION: The Cattaraugus Indian Reservation occupies a stretch of the coastline on Lake Erie. What operations do you carry out to protect that coastline, and what, if any, kinds of smuggling are taking place there? What is the level of cooperation between your agency and tribal law enforcement agencies? Do you have operations in any other Indian reservations in this area? How does this compare to the operations carried out by federal agencies at the Akwesasne (Mohawk) Reservation along the St. Lawrence River in eastern New York?

ANSWER: Some Native American Reservations, including the Cattaraugus Indian Reservation, present an enforcement challenge due to their cross border (straddling) location and the unique jurisdictional issues facing agencies that deal with them. The remote locations of some reservations and the reported desire of many residents of reservations to limit law enforcement presence exacerbate this challenge. Historical data indicates that reservations may be a conduit for the smuggling of illegal aliens, drugs, weapons and contraband. Although current Integrated Border Enforcement Teams have been effective in stemming a certain amount of illegal activity, it is far from complete and the Coast Guard continues to coordinate with local, tribal, state, federal and Canadian law enforcement agencies.

CITY OF BUFFALO
OFFICE OF THE MAYOR

ANTHONY M. MASIELLO
MAYOR

May 21, 2003

Hon. Mark E. Souder, Chair
Subcommittee on Criminal Justice, Drug Policy, and
Human Resources/Committee on Government Reform
2157 Rayburn House Office Building
Select Committee on Homeland Security
Washington, DC 20515

Dear Congressman Souder,

On behalf of the City of Buffalo, we thank you for the opportunity to attend the field hearing held in Niagara Falls, NY on Monday, May 19, 2003, concerning "Improving Security and Facilitating Commerce at the Northern Border."

Buffalo serves as the "gateway" to the International Peace Bridge and also, the International Railroad Bridge both crossing into Canada. The City of Buffalo is the 2nd largest City in the State of New York and is located within a 25 mile radius from Niagara Falls, NY, the home of the three (3) other northern border crossings, the Rainbow, Whirlpool (commercial) and Queenstown-Lewiston Bridges, thus we too, are concerned about the status of border security and law enforcement.

There was much discussion from the various leaders of the U.S. federal agencies primarily responsible for dealing with border protection and drug enforcement, specifically the Department of Homeland Security's Bureau of Customs and Border Protection and the Coast Guard, and also, the Department of Justice's Drug Enforcement Administration. Testimony and answers to questions posed by your committee reinforced the importance of communication between their agencies. "Interoperability" is also a concern of our local first responders. We need to ensure that all agencies can readily communicate with one another when disaster strikes within an area of "joint" jurisdictions.

As the local first responders within the City of Buffalo, we have assumed further duties in front line homeland defense in the war against terrorism. It is imperative that the federal government recognizes the need to dedicate personnel, equipment and training for infrastructure enhancements at the local response level, as well as the state and federal response levels. In light of our northern border's great resources and risk vulnerabilities, it is critical that we develop a coordinated, integrated, multi-agency response to any emergency or terrorist event(s) along our border.

We realize the challenges are many, therefore, we would like, for the record, to reinforce your message that while "examining border policies, we must of course also seek the input of representatives of the local community whose lives are affected by changes at the border." With this in mind, we encourage your Honorable Body to ensure that local responders are involved in the homeland security assessment and preparedness process, and also, as part of your mission, please include the needs of the first responders when bolstering the readiness of homeland security forces along our borders.

We stand together in our fight against terrorism and other homeland security threats.

We thank you for the time and effort you and your committee have dedicated to this vital matter of vigilance.

Sincerely,

Anthony M. Masiello, Mayor

Rocco J. Diina
Commissioner of Police

John W. Sniderhan
Disaster Coordinator

Calvin G. Worthy
Commissioner of Fire

cc: Congressional Hearing Attendees: Hon. D. Camp, Hon. J. Sweeney, Hon. J. Shadegg, Hon. J. Quinn, Hon. L. Slaughter, Hon. S. Jackson-Lee, Hon. L. Sanchez

2469 RAYBURN HOUSE OFFICE BUILDING
WASHINGTON, DC 20515
(202) 225-3615

3120 FEDERAL BUILDING
100 STATE STREET
ROCHESTER, NY 14614
(585) 232-4850

465 MAIN STREET, SUITE 105
BUFFALO, NY 14203
(716) 853-5813

1910 PINE AVENUE
NIAGARA FALLS, NY 14301
(716) 282-1274

E-mail: louiseny@mail.house.gov
Web: http://www.slaughter.house.gov

CONGRESS OF THE UNITED STATES
LOUISE M. SLAUGHTER
28TH DISTRICT, NEW YORK

COMMITTEE ON RULES
SUBCOMMITTEE ON
LEGISLATIVE AND BUDGET PROCESS

SELECT COMMITTEE ON
HOMELAND SECURITY

CONGRESSIONAL CAUCUS FOR
WOMEN'S ISSUES
DEMOCRATIC CO-CHAIR

CONGRESSIONAL ARTS CAUCUS
DEMOCRATIC CO-CHAIR

COMMITTEE ON ORGANIZATION,
STUDY, AND REVIEW

WHIP PARLIAMENTARY GROUP

COMMISSION ON SECURITY AND
COOPERATION IN EUROPE

On Monday, May 12th, I hosted a first responder forum that brought together a distinguished panel of federal Department of Homeland Security officials and first responders from throughout New York's 28th Congressional District. About one hundred police, fire, health and public officials participated in this first-of-a-kind event. The emphasis was on identifying the unique homeland security challenges encountered by first responders on the Northern Border. Attached are some policy and resource issues that were identified by first responders during the breakout sessions, which followed the presentations from Department of Homeland Security speakers.

Homeland Security Issues:

- Equipment—Police and fire officials expressed frustration with their ability to access vital homeland security equipment. The State determines the equipment needs of local firehouses with little or no input from local officials. Communities that were told years ago that a mobile response station was en route to their community have still not received this equipment.

  Equipment is disbursed by the State to local fire departments to cover only 10% of what the State determines is needed. Moreover, local communities have to absorb the maintenance and storage cost of highly technical equipment, such as HAZMAT suits, when the State provides equipment to local fire departments. They also expressed the need for mobile equipment for police cars. First responders from the City of Niagara Falls expressed frustration that the State has not provided a HAZMAT truck, which is essential to the City's ability to respond to a biological or nuclear attack. Officials from Niagara Falls and Lewiston discussed sharing a HAZMAT truck, since the communities are 10 miles apart.

- FIRE Grants—They expressed serious concerns about the future of the FEMA FIRE grant program. They appreciate that the FIRE grants allow small communities to secure resources and equipment directly from the federal government. At this time, it appears that the Department of Homeland Security will disburse the money to the States, who, in turn will disburse the funds as it sees fit.

- Training (and Certification)—Fire and police officials who have received equipment complain that access to training is an issue. They have assumed

2469 RAYBURN HOUSE OFFICE BUILDING
WASHINGTON, DC 20515
(202) 225-3615

3120 FEDERAL BUILDING
100 STATE STREET
ROCHESTER, NY 14614
(585) 232-4850

465 MAIN STREET, SUITE 105
BUFFALO, NY 14203
(716) 853-5813

1910 PINE AVENUE
NIAGARA FALLS, NY 14301
(716) 282-1274

E-mail: louiseny@mail.house.gov
Web: http://www.slaughter.house.gov

CONGRESS OF THE UNITED STATES
LOUISE M. SLAUGHTER
28TH DISTRICT, NEW YORK

COMMITTEE ON RULES
SUBCOMMITTEE ON
LEGISLATIVE AND BUDGET PROCESS

SELECT COMMITTEE ON
HOMELAND SECURITY

CONGRESSIONAL CAUCUS FOR
WOMEN'S ISSUES
DEMOCRATIC CO-CHAIR

CONGRESSIONAL ARTS CAUCUS
DEMOCRATIC CO-CHAIR

COMMITTEE ON ORGANIZATION,
STUDY, AND REVIEW

WHIP PARLIAMENTARY GROUP

COMMISSION ON SECURITY AND
COOPERATION IN EUROPE

more hazardous homeland security duties without proper training. The fire officials explained that they are unable to secure funding for training facilities since Federal Emergency Management Agency FIRE grants can only be used on equipment. Erie County is building a public safety building but needs funding for second phase-training facility.

Some first responders called for the establishment of a Federal Registry of First Responders. If an emergency happened in Ohio or even closer like Fort Erie, they suggested having a system in place where first responders who receive homeland security training are identified and mobilized. To ensure that proper procedures are adhered to, they suggest the issuance of picture identification cards that limit access to hazardous scenes. This would allow specially-trained first responders access to sensitive areas without waiting for clearance from federal officials in a disaster situation, when time is critical.

- Manpower—Local communities do not have adequate personnel to fully respond to a homeland security emergency. Personnel that were sent to participate in the joint homeland security taskforce have not been replaced. When the number of deployed reservists, who served as local responders, is taken into account, the staffing gap is compounded. The Niagara Falls Sheriff reports being down 10 reservists and numerous other officials who he "loaned out" to taskforces. In the public health arena, officials indicated that they have inadequate staffing resources, in the wake of anthrax, SARS, and other public health scares.

- Federal Financial Assistance—In the wake of September 11th, local communities along the U.S.-Canada border incurred great expense to secure the border. They ratcheted up their policing efforts and absorbed enormous overtime costs. More recently, changes in the nation's terror alert status bar have caused local communities to, again, incur expensive overtime costs.

  The current system, where counties competing against each other for the same federal money is problematic. They argue that when the State disburses money, it should go to where the biggest threats exist. The political officials would like to see Western New York designated a high priority area. Western New York has four of the seven top critical targets that warranted

2469 RAYBURN HOUSE OFFICE BUILDING
WASHINGTON, DC 20515
(202) 225-3615

3120 FEDERAL BUILDING
100 STATE STREET
ROCHESTER, NY 14614
(585) 232-4850

465 MAIN STREET, SUITE 105
BUFFALO, NY 14203
(716) 853-5813

1910 PINE AVENUE
NIAGARA FALLS, NY 14301
(716) 282-1274

E-mail: louiseny@mail.house.gov
Web: http://www.slaughter.house.gov

CONGRESS OF THE UNITED STATES
LOUISE M. SLAUGHTER
28TH DISTRICT, NEW YORK

COMMITTEE ON RULES
SUBCOMMITTEE ON
LEGISLATIVE AND BUDGET PROCESS

SELECT COMMITTEE ON
HOMELAND SECURITY

CONGRESSIONAL CAUCUS FOR
WOMEN'S ISSUES
DEMOCRATIC CO-CHAIR

CONGRESSIONAL ARTS CAUCUS
DEMOCRATIC CO-CHAIR

COMMITTEE ON ORGANIZATION,
STUDY, AND REVIEW

WHIP PARLIAMENTARY GROUP

COMMISSION ON SECURITY AND
COOPERATION IN EUROPE

heightened homeland security resources-- water, agriculture, power and an international border. It also has a high concentration of chemical plants.

The health officials also argued for a Regional Plan Coordinator, in recognition of the importance of coordinating city and county efforts. Officials from the Rochester area indicated that the Rochester Regional Health Association has already began a coordinated scheme where if one hospital goes down during an emergency, others can take over.

Representatives from the Red Cross indicated that they would like to be informed of funding opportunities at the same time as local public health officials. Health officials expressed the view that the country would benefit far better from a strong public health system and not simply a limited bio-terrorism system. They also expressed frustration with the size of existing grants. One hospital was eligible and received a $5,000 grant under the Medicaid Retrospective Reimbursement System (MRRS), but it was used to build a decontamination shelter that cost $12,000. Other hospitals, such as Park Ridge Hospital in Rochester, is not eligible for many grants because it is not classified as an acute care center.

Among all of the groups, there is great concern that the State would somehow manage to keep most of the money or send it to New York City. They asked for assistance in how to access federal money as soon as possible so that they have enough time to apply for grants.

All four groups also indicated that they needed help with grant writing and talked about hiring one grant writer for several localities. There was a consensus that there is a need to streamline the process to make it easier for locals to access the funding.

- Communications— All four groups identified the lack of adequate communications equipment that is interoperable on the Federal, State, county, and local level as integral to their efforts. Today, local first responders lack equipment and access to a radio system that connects the counties. In some communities, fire and police departments can talk but they do not have a mechanism to talk with U.S. Border Patrol, state public utilities or local health

2469 RAYBURN HOUSE OFFICE BUILDING
WASHINGTON, DC 20515
(202) 225-3615

3120 FEDERAL BUILDING
100 STATE STREET
ROCHESTER, NY 14614
(585) 232-4850

465 MAIN STREET, SUITE 105
BUFFALO, NY 14203
(716) 853-5813

1910 PINE AVENUE
NIAGARA FALLS, NY 14301
(716) 282-1274

E-mail: louiseny@mail.house.gov
Web: http://www.slaughter.house.gov

CONGRESS OF THE UNITED STATES
LOUISE M. SLAUGHTER
28TH DISTRICT, NEW YORK

COMMITTEE ON RULES
SUBCOMMITTEE ON
LEGISLATIVE AND BUDGET PROCESS

SELECT COMMITTEE ON
HOMELAND SECURITY

CONGRESSIONAL CAUCUS FOR
WOMEN'S ISSUES
DEMOCRATIC CO-CHAIR

CONGRESSIONAL ARTS CAUCUS
DEMOCRATIC CO-CHAIR

COMMITTEE ON ORGANIZATION,
STUDY, AND REVIEW

WHIP PARLIAMENTARY GROUP

COMMISSION ON SECURITY AND
COOPERATION IN EUROPE

officials. Public health officials argued for the establishment of a reliable communication system using voice data for health care professionals to communicate amongst themselves and a real time alert system for public health officials to notify the public about health emergencies.

Police and fire officials criticized the State for failing to turn over the state surcharge on wireless devices to the localities to deploy "enhanced 9-11 services" and a statewide wireless communications system. As it stands now, the eight counties in Western New York cannot communicate immediately if there is a disaster. The village of Lewiston heard about the September 11th attacks on CNN. This community lies right in the middle of a chemical waste dump, international border crossing and a power plant. Lewiston is also responsible for arresting illegal aliens that have managed to get into the country. Localities that want to deploy this technology have to pay for it on their own.

- Inclusion in State and Federal Homeland Security Discussions—A majority of the fire officials expressed frustration that they are not included in the State and Federal priority-setting process. As first responders, they argue that they have expertise as to the nature and scope of the security issues in their community and are best situated to know what resources would be needed on the local level. Officials from Rochester expressed concern that the State was working with an out-dated security plan submitted by Monroe County. They feel they have no forum to raise their security needs.

MAY-16-2003 03:26P FROM: TO:8536347 P:1/2

Upper Mountain Fire Company

839 Moyer Road
Lewiston, NY 14092
(716) 297-0330
(716) 297-1074 (FAX)
Established 1959

Congresswomen Louise Slaughter
465 Main Street
Buffalo, New York 14203

May 16, 2003

Re: Homeland Security Issues.

Dear Congresswoman Slaughter:

Since its inception in the late 1950's, the Upper Mountain Volunteer Fire Company has been charged with providing fire and EMS protection to one of the greatest assets of the State of New York, the New York Power Authority. This vital energy generating facility is essential to the very livelihood of not only the citizens of our state but also the citizens of neighboring states. It is, and remains, an element essential to the economic stability of the State of New York. The loss of this facility would have a disastrous effect upon our country.

Unfortunately, the construction of this facility transformed this rural community, into a prime Cold War Era Nuclear target and now, according to many; including NYPA, a prime terrorists target. One need only to travel the public roadways in this community to see the millions of dollars that NYPA has expended to deter the impact of a terrorist assault on the facility. This transformation in itself exemplifies and serves as visual testimony to the on going Public Safety threat faced by this community/ a rural community of limited financial means that is charged with an enormous task. A task we might add that is not financially assisted by this facility. Needless to say an assault upon this facility would have a disastrous effect.

Less than a half a mile north of the Power Authority is the international border crossing for commercial traffic entering Lewiston New York. Daily thousands of trucks and cars enter or leave this Country by way of the Lewiston-Queenston Bridge. Each of these vehicles crosses over the Authority's forebay coming within hundreds of feet of the facility's generators and switchyard. One only needs to visit this border checkpoint to see the extremes that have been taken to deter an assault and enhance detection; all of this aimed at preventing as assault on the project. We, as first responders, must respond when and if this assault comes. To this end we need to be prepared.

It is in this vein that we are seeking your assistance. Our homeland security and protection needs are great. They can no longer be met solely by town financial assistance, nor by our annual door to door campaign, or traditional fund raising events.

We welcome the opportunity to sit with you and your staff to discuss our concerns, and ask that you assist us in meeting the challenges facing upon this small rural community.

Very Truly Yours

John C. Malinchock
Assist.Chief Upper Mountain Fire Co.
Lewiston, New York

Jonathan Schultz
Captain Upper Mountain Fire Co
Lewiston, New York

cc. Joseph Passanese Chief

Niagara Interfaith Chaplaincy Inc.
The Rev. Patrick J. Bradley, Executive Director
P.O. Box 4075, Niagara Falls, NY 14304
Phone: (716) 283-8022 Pager: (716) 443-3424
E-mail: pjbradley@juno.com
State Representative - International Conference of Police Chaplains
Member - New York State Association of Fire Chaplains
Member - International Critical Incident Stress Foundation

May 18, 2003

Hon. Louise M. Slaughter
2469 Rayburn House Office Building
Washington, DC 20515-3228

Dear Congresswoman Slaughter:

As executive director of an organization that provides services to more than a half-dozen law enforcement agencies (local, county and state) in Niagara County, New York, and as state representative for the International Conference of Police Chaplains, the world's premier organization for the training, certification and support of law enforcement chaplains, allow me to convey heartfelt thanks for your continued interest in Homeland Security issues, particularly as they affect those of us living along the U.S.-Canada border.

I am told there was a fruitful exchange of concerns and ideas during last week's forum for local first responders and officials from the Department of Homeland Security and the U.S. Bureau of Customs and Border Protection, a forum you hosted in neighboring Erie County. I am confident the hearings being held today in Niagara Falls by the Homeland Security Committee's Subcommittee on Infrastructure and Border Security will be every bit as productive as representatives from both sides of the border meet to pursue ways to work together for our mutual safety and benefit.

During those hearings, I expect you will hear that law enforcement resources have been stretched painfully thin in Western New York since the September 2001 terrorist attacks as departments in our cash-strapped municipalities are continually asked to do more with less. In many cases their ranks have been thinned, not only by budgetary limits imposed by elected officials fighting to limit tax increases but by the loss of many highly trained and qualified officers to active duty assignments with their military Reserve and National Guard units.

At the same time, the scope of their operations has grown significantly as they have been required to assume added responsibility, and to exercise increased diligence and vigilance in the course of their duties as they patrol a geographic area that includes a U.S. Air Force Reserve station; two international airports, a host of chemical plants; the Niagara Power Project, one of the largest hydropower plants in the United States; and four international bridges.

These professionals will share their concerns about a number of other security issues, as well, and will make numerous requests for the resources they need to perform their jobs and keep us safe. I hope you and the members of Homeland Security Committee and its Subcommittee on Infrastructure and Border Security will make every effort to fulfill those requests.

What I am almost certain you will not hear them talk about is the impact such dangerous work has on the dedicated people who perform it.

Law enforcement officers work each day in a dangerous and stress-filled environment that over the course of a career can take a tremendous toll.

Consider these statistics:

- Dr. Steve Douglas, longtime psychologist for the Columbus Police Department in Columbus, Ohio, said at a recent International Conference of Police Chaplains seminar that the first-marriage divorce rate for police officers is approaching 85 percent.
- According to Dr. Ronald J. Burke, a researcher at York University in Ontario, Canada, 40 percent of U.S. police officers report at least one episode of physical aggression during a conflict with his or her spouse/partner during the previous year.
- A 1998 study published in the journal "Addictions" reported that in a survey of 852 law enforcement officers, 48 percent of the males and 40 percent of the females reported excessive drinking. About the same percentages reporting excessive eating.
- The Central Florida Police Stress Unit Inc. reports that an officer in the United States is killed in the line of duty every 56 hours.
- Last year, police suffered 182 line of duty deaths. In 2001, 232 officers died in the line of duty. Seventy-two of deaths occurred as a result of the Sept. 11 terrorist attacks.
- According to the National P.O.L.I.C.E. Suicide Foundation, a police officer takes his or her own life every 22 hours in the United States. The numbers of deaths due to suicide are two to three times the number of line of duty deaths among law enforcement agencies and emergency workers.

Law enforcement personnel are trained to take command of situations and bring them under control, arrest law breakers and get help for those who need it while keeping their personal feelings under control at all times. Because this mindset is so deeply entrenched, the toughest part of staying healthy for the average officer is admitting when he or she has a problem. The second biggest roadblock is an ingrained resistance to asking for help.

The workplace environment officers have endured since Sept. 11, 2001, has exacerbated these problems. Increased overtime has resulted in heightened fatigue, which degrades job performance, and increased separation from home and family, with subsequent increases in relational distress.

Yet, officers whose mental and emotional needs are addressed on an ongoing basis can be expected to demonstrate lower rates of illness, divorce, substance abuse, domestic violence and suicide, all of which degrade on-the-job effectiveness, ruin or end lives and careers, and cost taxpayers uncounted thousands of dollars a year.

My primary concern is this: We are demanding law enforcement personnel do more to protect us, yet we are doing precious little to take proper care of them. Despite the known advantages of providing them with ongoing stress management services (see Issues and Practices in Criminal Justice, March 1997: "Developing a Law Enforcement Stress Program for Officers and Their Families," U.S. Department of Justice, Office of Justice Programs, National Institute of Justice) most departments do not offer such services on an ongoing basis.

Some departments have programs using contract agencies that offer initial stress management orientation and periodic refresher instruction along with peer support personnel training. These contract agencies (examples in your congressional district include the Catch a Falling Star Law Enforcement Employee Assistance Program in Lancaster, Employee Resources in Buffalo and CISM Perspectives in Rochester) also respond to critical incidents such as mass casualty incidents and officer-involved shootings.

Other departments (such as the New York State Police) offer in-house programs using specially trained and highly qualified agency members who are nonetheless often asked to serve multiple sites covering a wide geographic area.

Many departments have no stress management programs at all.

It goes without saying that the men and women behind the badge are the most precious resource we have in maintaining homeland security. It is critical, both morally and from a performance standpoint, that we make every effort to keep them in the best possible condition -- physically, mentally and emotionally. It makes fiscal sense, too, in that it is much less costly to help an officer who needs it and keep that officer on the job than it is to replace that same officer.

Yet, there are precious few federal resources available to perform that important task. In

1992, for example, Niagara Interfaith Chaplaincy filed a joint application with three regions of the New York State Park Police, an agency with no stress management program, for me and three regional commanders to attend the U.S. Department of Justice/National Institute of Justice's Eastern Regional Symposium for the Corrections and Law Enforcement Family Support (CLEFS) Program. Our intent was to use the material presented at the symposium as the basis for initiating a stress management program in those regions.

Due to an overwhelming response, our application was not accepted and a golden opportunity was squandered.

I hope that as a member of the House Select Committee on Homeland Security and the Homeland Security Committee's Subcommittee on Infrastructure and Border Security you will insist on proper care for the members all law enforcement agencies tasked with providing homeland security on all levels. These agencies will be asking for money to provide their members with needed training. I ask you to make the provision of ongoing stress management programming a mandatory component for the use of federal funds set aside for training purposes.

The better we care for our law enforcement personnel, the better they will be able to perform for us.

Thank you for your attention to this vital matter.

Respectfully yours,

Patrick J. Bradley

Free And Secure Trade

***FAST* Overview**

The *FAST* program is a bilateral initiative between the United States and Canada designed to ensure security and safety while enhancing the economic prosperity of both countries. In developing this program, Canada and the United States have agreed to harmonize, to the maximum extent possible, their commercial processes for clearance of commercial shipments at the border. This will promote free and secure trade by using common risk-management principles, supply chain security, industry partnership, and advanced technology to improve the efficiency of screening and clearing commercial traffic at our shared border.

***FAST* Objectives**

FAST is an ambitious program both in terms of its scope and its implementation date. For the U.S. and Canada the initiative's objectives promise to revolutionize the processing of transborder trade:

1. The program aims to increase the integrity of supply chain management by offering expedited clearance to carriers and importers enrolled in Customs Trade Partnership Against Terrorism (C-TPAT), or Canada's Partners in Protection (PIP).
2. It's designed to streamline and to integrate registration processes for drivers, carriers, and importers; minimizing paperwork and ensuring only low risk participants are enrolled as members.
3. The initiative seeks to expedite clearance of low risk transborder shipments by reducing Customs information requirements, dedicating lanes at major crossings to *FAST* participants, using common technology, and physically examining cargo transported by these low risk clients at the lowest levels possible.
4. The program is a catalyst for both Customs administrations to integrate and enhance technologies—transponders employed on both sides of the border, for example—which would make it even easier to clear low risk shipments, and which would mitigate the cost of program participation for *FAST* partners.

***FAST* Benefits**

FAST approved highway carriers will benefit from:

1. Dedicated lanes (where available) for greater speed and efficiency in the clearance of *FAST* transborder shipments.
2. Reduced number of examinations for continued compliance with

Customs *FAST* requirements.
3. A strong and ongoing partnership with the Canadian (PIP) and U.S. Customs (C-TPAT) administrations.
4. Enhanced supply chain security and safety while protecting the economic prosperity of both countries.
5. The knowledge that they're carrying shipments for a C-TPAT approved importer.
6. A head start for the upcoming modifications to *FAST* that will expand eligible electronic cargo release methods. The *FAST* processing of Pre Arrival Processing System (PAPS) shipments is expected to commence within the next year.

<u>*FAST* Inauguration</u>

The initial phase of *FAST* for U.S. Bound commercial shipments, which began in December 2002, will be available for qualifying commercial shipments at the following U.S./Canadian ports:

1. Blaine - Douglas
2. Detroit - Windsor
3. Port Huron - Sarnia
4. Buffalo - Fort Erie
5. Lewiston - Queenston
6. Champlain - Lacolle

<u>Qualifications for *FAST* Participants</u>

FAST is a harmonized clearance process for known low-risk shipments. Thus, any truck using *FAST* lane processing must be a C-TPAT approved carrier, carrying qualifying goods from a U.S. Customs-Trade Partnership Against Terrorism (C-TPAT) approved importer, and the driver in the possession of a valid *FAST*-Commercial Driver Card. *FAST* processing is based upon advanced electronic transmission of information. The following are the key components:

1. **Importer Registration:** Importers will complete separate applications to the Customs administrations in the United States and Canada. Importers authorized to use the *FAST* program for clearance into the United States will have a demonstrated history of complying with all relevant legislative and regulatory requirements, and will have made a commitment to security enhancing business practices as required by C-TPAT.

2. **Carrier Registration:** Carriers will complete the *FAST* Highway Carrier Application Process requirements that include corporate information, a security profile, and a written Highway Carrier Agreement. In order to qualify for *FAST* Highway Carrier membership

into the U.S. and Canada, two separate applications must be submitted to each country's respective *FAST* Processing Centers.

Each country will perform an independent risk assessment and each country will issue independent approvals for participation. For the United States, a *FAST* approved carrier will have met all aspects of C-TPAT through the *FAST* registration process.

3. **Commercial Driver Application:** Drivers will complete a single *FAST* Commercial Driver Application for the U.S. and Canada. The application will be risk assessed by the customs and immigration services of both countries. Applicants identified as low risk will report to an enrollment center where they will be interviewed, have their original identification and citizenship documents reviewed, fingerprinted and have a digital photo taken. Low-risk applicants will then be issued a *FAST* – Commercial Driver Card.

***FAST Commercial Driver* Enrollment Centers**

FAST enrollment centers can be found at the following locations:

1. Blaine, Washington
2. Detroit, Michigan
3. Port Huron, Michigan
4. Buffalo, New York
5. Champlain, New York

Cargo Release Method(s)

The two cargo release methods for *FAST* shipments are the National Customs Automated Prototype (NCAP) and the Pre-Arrival Processing System (PAPS). NCAP/*FAST* processing for *FAST* began in December, 2002. The *FAST* processing of PAPS shipments is expected to start next year.

1. ***FAST***: *FAST* is the first completely paperless cargo release mechanism put into place by U.S. Customs. This paperless processing is achieved through electronic data transmissions and transponder technology. *FAST* is highly automated and allows for the expedited release of highly compliant cargo from major importers, reducing congestion at our land borders.

2. **Pre Arrival Processing System (PAPS) -**The Pre-Arrival Processing System (PAPS) is a U.S. Customs ACS (Automated Commercial System) border cargo release mechanism that utilizes barcode technology to expedite the release of commercial shipments while still processing each shipment through Border Cargo Selectivity (BCS) and the Automated Targeting System (ATS).

Each PAPS shipment requires a unique barcode label, which the carrier attaches to the invoice and the truck manifest while the merchandise is still in Canada. The barcode consists of the Standard Carrier Alpha Code (SCAC) and Pro-Bill number. This information is then faxed ahead to the Customs broker in the U.S., who prepares a BCS entry in ACS. Upon the truck's arrival at the border, the Customs Inspector scans the barcode, which automatically retrieves the entry information from ACS. If no examination is required, the Inspector then releases the truck from the primary booth, reducing the carrier's wait time and easing congestion at the U.S. border.

Additional Information

Additional information can be found on the Customs web site at www.customs.gov by typing *FAST* under the search criteria. In addition, you can call one of the designated *FAST* ports and ask for a *FAST* representative.

Pre Arrival Processing System (PAPS)

The Pre-Arrival Processing System (PAPS) is a U.S. Bureau of Customs and Border Protection border cargo release mechanism that utilizes barcode technology to expedite the release of commercial shipments while still processing each shipment through Border Cargo Selectivity (BCS) and the Automated Targeting System (ATS).

Each PAPS shipment requires a unique barcode label, which the carrier attaches to the invoice and the truck manifest while the merchandise is still in Canada. The barcode consists of the U.S. Standard Carrier Alpha Code (SCAC) and Pro-Bill number. This information is then faxed ahead to the Customs broker in the U.S., who prepares a BCS entry in ACS. Upon the truck's arrival at the border, the Customs Inspector scans the barcode, which automatically retrieves the entry information from ACS. If no examination is required, the Inspector then releases the truck from the primary booth, reducing the carrier's wait time and easing congestion at the U.S. border.

How to use PAPS

1) To obtain your U.S. Standard Carrier Alpha Code (SCAC), contact the National Motor Freight Traffic Association (NMFTA) at (703) 838-1868 or at www.NMFTA.org

2) Fax a copy of your NMFTA letter of notification with your assigned SCAC to:

   Customs and Border Protection
   Office of Applications Development
   ATTN: Charles A. Bennett
   (703) 921-7173 (Fax number)

3) Creating a PAPS barcode:
   Some carriers develop their own and others use commercial printers. Remember, the SCAC, Number, and Check Digit should be continuous without spaces or dashes.

   Bar Code Label Design
   2 7/8" wide by 1 1/4" high
   SCAC and PRO must be less than 16 characters
   Medium density code 3 of 9

4) To ensure barcode compatibility with Customs technology, a sample of your PAPS designated barcode must be tested at the ports of entry where PAPS entries will be processed. This action must be completed prior to the processing of PAPS transactions.

5) Inform your Customs Broker of your intent to use PAPS and acquire their broker/filer code. Also, establish fax procedures to transmit entry information, which will includes, invoice, SCAC, and pro bill number and an agreement on the amount of advanced notice needed for submitting ABI entry information.

   Important Note: PAPS is for U.S. bound commercial vehicles and is NOT INTERCHANGEABLE with the Canadian PARS System which is designed for Canadian bound commercial traffic.

Print this Page

Close this Window

Printer Friendly Version Of:
http://www.customs.gov/xp/cgov/import/commercial_enforcement/ctpat/fast/cd_program/fast_commercial.xml
Printed: Tue May 13 14:18:42 EDT 2003

U.S. /Canada FAST Commercial Driver Program

Beginning in November 2002, commercial truck drivers who transport goods across U.S./Canadian border may apply for membership in the Free and Secure Trade (FAST) Commercial Driver program.

This program will allow commercial drivers to use one application form to apply for expedited U.S. /Canadian Customs and Immigration processing while transporting qualifying commercial shipments at the U.S. / Canadian border.

For detailed eligibility requirements and application information, please refer to the documents below:

FAST Commercial Driver Information and Application Instructions (PDF)
Contains information and application instructions necessary to complete the FAST Commercial Driver Application.

FAST Commercial Driver Application (PDF)

All FAST Commercial Driver applications must be sent to:

FAST Commercial Driver Program
4551 Zimmerman Avenue
P.O. Box 66
Niagara Falls, ON L2E 6T1
Canada

For difficulties accessing information due to a disability, or any questions regarding C-TPAT or FAST, contact industry.partnership@customs.treas.gov

Commercial Driver

Information and Application Form

FAST
EXPRES

Government of Canada / Gouvernement du Canada

United States of America

RC4317(E)

La version française de cette publication est intitulée *FAST – Guide du participant.*

FAST Commercial Driver Program

Free And Secure Trade (FAST) Commercial Driver Program is the result of the Smart Border Declaration – 30 Point Action Plan and is a harmonized program involving the Canada Customs and Revenue Agency (CCRA), Citizenship and Immigration Canada (CIC), the U.S. Customs Service (USCS), and the U.S. Immigration and Naturalization Service (USINS).

What are the benefits?

If you are approved to participate in the FAST Commercial Driver Program, you will receive a card to use at the border that will allow you to:

- use FAST dedicated lanes in Canada and the U.S. (where available);
- cross the border with accelerated customs and immigration processing; and,
- transport eligible goods for FAST approved carriers and importers.

Who qualifies?

You may qualify to participate in the program if you are a citizen or permanent resident of the U.S. or Canada, age 18 or over and possess a valid driver's license. You must be admissible to Canada and the U.S. under applicable immigration laws. However, you **may not** qualify if you:

- provide false or incomplete information on your application;
- have been convicted of a criminal offence;
- have been found in violation of customs or immigration law; or
- fail to meet other requirements of the FAST Commercial Driver Program.

Both countries must approve your application. If you do not meet the requirements of both countries, your application will be denied.

How do I apply?

Your participation in this program is strictly voluntary. If you complete the attached application form, we will use the information you provided to determine your eligibility. If you meet initial requirements, you will be invited to visit the enrollment centre for final processing. During this stage, we will:

- review the information you provided on your application form to ensure it is accurate and valid;
- review original documents such as proof of citizenship, residency, work permits, and/or visas;
- take a full set of fingerprints;
- take your photo for your FAST Commercial Driver card;
- explain the terms and conditions of the FAST Commercial Driver Program; and
- following appropriate background checks, you will be notified if you have qualified.

Completing the application

Each person who wants to participate in the FAST Commercial Driver Program must fill out a separate application form.

The following sections give details about certain parts of the application form.

Preferred Language – Indicate English or French. Canadian officials will correspond with you in the language of your choice. U.S. officials will correspond with you in English.

Check the box that applies – *First time applicant* or *Renewal or Replacement.*

Section A – Personal Information

Other names used – If you have ever changed your name (including by marriage), provide the previous name(s) you have used.

Citizenship and Residence – Indicate whether you are a citizen of Canada, the United States, or another country. Be sure to indicate all countries of which you are a citizen or national (i.e. you are a dual national). Check the box that corresponds with your country of permanent residence.

Proof of Citizenship and Residency – Acceptable proof of Canadian or U.S. citizenship includes birth certificate and photo identification, a passport or citizenship certificate or card, a certificate of registration of birth abroad, or a certificate of naturalization. Proof of Canadian or U.S. permanent residency includes a record of landing in Canada, a valid Canadian permanent resident card or a valid U.S. permanent resident card. Please provide copies of any visas you are required to present. Be prepared to provide proof that your citizenship, residency and immigration status are as stated on the application form.

Two photocopies of proof of citizenship and residency, along with two photocopies of your valid drivers license, must be sent with your application form to the FAST Commercial Driver program processing centre. Failure to do so will result in the application being returned to you. However, if the document indicates that it is a violation to copy it, please note this on your application and bring the original with you to your interview.

You will need to bring all the original documents required for your admission to the U.S. and Canada to the enrollment office to be verified as part of the interview process.

Section B – Address history for the last 5 years

You must provide details of your address history for the past 5 years. Use the spaces provided, starting with your current address. Attach a separate sheet, if necessary.

Section C – Employment history for the last 5 years

You must provide details of your employment history for the past 5 years. Use the spaces provided, starting with your current employer. Attach a separate sheet, if necessary.

Lack of employment will not disqualify you from participation, if you are otherwise admissible to the U.S. and Canada, and meet all other program requirements.

To use a FAST card you must be transporting eligible goods for a FAST approved carrier and importer.

Section D – Additional information

Indicate any convictions for offences in any country for which you have not received a pardon for example, alcohol related offences. You must also indicate any immigration or customs violations. For Canadian background checks on admissibility, you may be questioned with regards to offences committed outside Canada, pardons granted by countries other than Canada and deemed rehabilitation. For U.S. background checks, you may be questioned about your full criminal history, including arrests or pardons.

You must also indicate if you have ever applied to CIC for rehabilitation.

You must also indicate any waivers of inadmissibility you have been issued by the USINS.

Section E – Certification

The laws that protect personal information collected by government agencies differ in Canada and the United States. You should read the U.S. and Canadian privacy statements and the certification statement on the application form carefully. You must sign and date the certification statement.

The U.S. *Privacy Act* applies to U.S. citizens and U.S. permanent residents, including Canadian and other nationals who fall into either of these two categories. The Canadian *Privacy Act* applies to all persons applying to the Canadian portion of the program.

Section F – Fee payment

For every application there is a non-refundable fee for the FAST Commercial Driver Program of $80.00 Canadian **or** U.S. $50.00. Program participation will be valid for a five-year period. This fee is equally divided by the two countries and includes the existing U.S. $25.00 application fee for a land border alternative inspection program as well as the $40.00 Canadian application fee.

You must include a money order or a certified cheque for the total amount in Canadian or U.S. dollars made payable to the *Receiver General for Canada*. As an option you may provide a Visa or MasterCard number with your signature.

Do not send cash.

How do I declare goods?

As a FAST Commercial Driver participant, you must declare all goods you are importing whenever you cross the border into the U.S. or Canada.

If you are entering the U.S. and are importing goods for your personal use, you must make an oral declaration to the officer in the booth. For more information, U.S. residents should refer to the U.S. pamphlet called ***Know Before You Go*** and Canadian residents visiting the U.S. should see the publication called ***Visiting the United States***.

If you are entering the U.S. and have goods to declare in excess of your personal exemption, you must use the regular lane.

If you are entering Canada and are importing goods for your personal use that do not exceed your personal exemption, you must make a verbal declaration to the officer in the booth. For more information about importing goods into Canada, Canadian residents should see the CCRA pamphlet called ***I Declare*** and U.S. residents should see the pamphlet called ***Customs Information for Visitors to Canada and Seasonal Residents.***

If you are entering either Canada or the U.S. and have goods to declare in excess of your personal exemption, you must use the regular lane.

Note: Canadian residents have the option of obtaining ***Traveller Declaration Cards*** (TDCs) that can be presented any time you cross into Canada using the FAST lane. The card must be completed before arriving in Canada. When you arrive, hand your TDC to the officer in the booth. If you exceed your personal exemption, the duties and tax owing will be charged to your credit card.

Are there restrictions on the goods I can import for personal use?

- You cannot import controlled, restricted, or prohibited firearms or weapons, including mace, pepper spray, and stun guns;
- you cannot import controlled, restricted, or prohibited goods, animals, or plants. This includes controlled, restricted, or prohibited substances, endangered animals or species, and restricted fruits and vegetables. For more information, see the pamphlets mentioned previously; and,

- if you bring or carry more than US $10,000 in currency and monetary instruments into or out of the U.S., you must use the regular lane and make a declaration to U.S. Customs.

What else do I need to know?

The card is valid for a period of 5 years provided you continue to meet all the terms and conditions of this program.

Only approved FAST Commercial Drivers can use FAST dedicated lanes (where available). As a FAST Commercial Driver, you remain subject to compliance and enforcement checks at any time you cross the border.

If you use the FAST dedicated lane, everyone in the vehicle must be in possession of a valid FAST commercial driver card and transporting eligible goods for a FAST approved carrier and importer.

We will take a full set of fingerprints to perform criminal records checks. This biometric will be shared with other government and law enforcement agencies. In addition, any personal information you provide will be shared with other government and law enforcement agencies.

Your application will be denied if you do not meet both Canadian and U.S. requirements for admission into the FAST Commercial Driver Program.

Your FAST Commercial Driver card is not a travel document that authorizes your admission to the U.S. or Canada. Your FAST Commercial Driver card validation and expiration date will depend on your underlying citizenship or immigration status for each country. Your immigration status must be valid at all times, and you must possess appropriate immigration and identity documents in addition to your FAST Commercial Driver card. These may include your passport (required for some countries), birth certificate, visa, permanent resident card, employment authorization, work permit, and other related documents.

Penalties for the Provision of False Information

The failure to provide true, accurate and complete information in an application to the FAST Commercial Driver Program may result in denial of your application. Penalties are provided by law for knowingly and willfully falsifying or concealing a material fact, or using any false document in submitting your application. A false representation also may result in the denial of this and any other application you may make for any benefit under U.S. Immigration laws.

U.S. FAST Lane Conditions

Applicants acknowledge and agree that if they violate any conditions of this program, or any law or regulation of any Federal Inspection Service, or are otherwise determined to be inadmissible to the U.S., their participation in this program may be revoked and they may be subject to other applicable sanctions. Such sanctions may include, but are not limited to, criminal prosecution, removal proceedings, imposition of civil monetary penalties, and seizures of merchandise and vehicles. Conditions by which applicants must abide include, but are not limited to, the following:

a) adherence to all state, federal, and local laws regarding the importation of alcohol and agriculture products, possession and importation of controlled substances, and all other laws and regulations under the jurisdiction of any federal agency.

b) adherence to all requirements of the *Immigration and Nationality Act*, as amended, U.S. Customs regulations, and all Federal Inspection Service regulations regarding documentary requirements.

If you violate the terms and conditions of this program, we may cancel your privileges and you may face fines, penalties, and criminal charges. We will strictly enforce the law.

Canadian FAST Lane Conditions

Applicants acknowledge and agree that if they violate any conditions of this program, or are otherwise determined to be inadmissible to Canada, their participation in this program may be revoked and they may be subject to other applicable sanctions.

Mail your application and fee payment to the address found on the application form (attached).

For more information

Please contact the FAST Commercial Driver Program processing centres at:

4551 Zimmerman Avenue
P.O. Box 66
Niagara Falls ON L2E 6T1
Canada

FAST Driver Registration Office
50 South Main St., Suite 100R
St. Albans, VT. 05478
U. S. A.

Or visit our web sites at:

www.ccra-adrc.gc.ca

www.Customs.gov

Think Recycling!

Printed in Canada

Government of Canada Gouvernement du Canada

U.S. Department of Justice
Immigration and Naturalization Service

Please type or print

FAST COMMERCIAL DRIVER APPLICATION

1a. ☐ First time applicant ☐ Renewal or Replacement | 1b. Border crossing most frequently used | 1c. Preferred language ▶ ☐ English ☐ French

SECTION A - PERSONAL INFORMATION

2. Last name | 3. First name | 4. Middle name (in full)

5. Other names used (e.g., maiden name, former name) | Nickname | 6. Gender ☐ Male ☐ Female | 7. Date of birth Year Month Day

8. Place of birth ▶ City | Province/State | Country

9. Citizenship (Check all that apply.)
☐ Canadian citizen ☐ U.S. citizen ☐ Other (Please specify) ____________

10. Residence
☐ Canada ☐ United States

11. Proof of citizenship/residency/immigration status (Attach two copies of proof of citizenship, residency and drivers license.)

☐ Birth certificate No. ____________ ☐ Passport No. ____________ ____________ Country of issuance Year Month Day (Expiry date)

☐ Citizenship card No. ____________ ☐ Permanent resident document No. ____________ ☐ U.S. Alien Registration No. ____________

☐ Other ▶ Type of document ____________ No. ____________ Year Month Day (Expiry date)

☐ Drivers licence No. ____________ ____________ State/Province of issue Year Month Day (Expiry date)

SECTION B - ADDRESS HISTORY FOR THE LAST 5 YEARS

12. Current address As of: Year Month | 13. Street address | 14. Apt. | 15. City

16. Province/State | 17. Postal/Zip code | 18. Country | 19. Home telephone ( ) - | 20. Business telephone / Cell phone number ( ) - Ext.

Mailing address if different from residential address

21. Street address | 22. Apt.

23. City | 24. Province/State | 25. Postal/Zip code | 26. Country

Previous residential addresses if current residence is less than five years (attach a separate sheet if necessary).

27. From: Year Month To: Year Month | 28. Street address | 29. Apt.

30. City | 31. Province/State | 32. Postal/Zip code | 33. Country

34. From: Year Month To: Year Month | 35. Street address | 36. Apt.

37. City | 38. Province/State | 39. Postal/Zip code | 40. Country

41. From: Year Month To: Year Month | 42. Street address | 43. Apt.

44. City | 45. Province/State | 46. Postal/Zip code | 47. Country

Continued on reverse ▶

Send your completed form and photocopies of the required documents to:

FAST Commercial Driver Program

4551 Zimmerman Avenue
P.O. Box 66
Niagara Falls, Ontario
L2E 6T1
CANADA

SECTION C - EMPLOYMENT HISTORY FOR THE LAST 5 YEARS

48. Current employer — From: Year / Month — To: Year / Month
49. Employer's name
50. Street address
51. Apt.
52. City
53. Province/State
54. Postal/Zip code
55. Country
56. Telephone number ( ) - Ext.
57. Occupation

Previous Employer name and address if current employer is less than five years (attach a separate sheet if necessary).

58. From: Year / Month — To: Year / Month
59. Employer's name
60. Street address
61. Apt.
62. City
63. Province/State
64. Postal/Zip code
65. Country

SECTION D - ADDITIONAL INFORMATION

66.

Have you ever been convicted of an offence in any country for which you have not received a pardon? ☐ No ☐ Yes

Have you ever received a waiver of inadmissibity to the U.S. from the USINS? ☐ No ☐ Yes

Have you ever applied to the Minister of Citizenship and Immigration Canada (CIC) for rehabilitation? ☐ No ☐ Yes

Have you ever been found in violation of customs or immigration laws? ☐ No ☐ Yes

If you have answered *YES*, please give details; ____________

For U.S. background checks, you may be questioned by a U.S. Officer about your full criminal history, including arrests and pardons.

SECTION E - CERTIFICATION

67.

I certify that all information given on this application, and in support of this application, was provided voluntarily and is true and complete. I understand that any information on this application, including any supporting documentation, background information, and biometric data will be shared among Customs and Immigration authorities in both Canada and the U.S. and among law enforcement and other government agencies in accordance with applicable laws. I certify that I have read, understood, and agree to abide by all conditions required for use of the FAST program, including all instructions and notices accompanying this application.

Applicant ▶ Name (print) | Signature | Date

U.S. PRIVACY ACT STATEMENT

The authority to collect the information on this application, any supporting documentation, fingerprints, and other requested information is contained in Titles 8 and 19 of the U.S. Code and corresponding regulations. Furnishing the information on this form is voluntary; however, failure to provide all the requested information may result in the delay of a final decision or denial of your request. The information collected will be used to make a determination on your application. It may also be provided to other government agencies (Federal, state, local, and/or foreign) as permitted under the Privacy Act of 1974, 5 U.S.C. § 552a (2002) and other applicable law. All applicants are subject to a check of criminal information databases and other immigration and customs databases in order to determine eligibility for this program.

CANADA'S PRIVACY STATEMENT

The information you provide on this form, including supporting documentation and biometric data, is collected under the *Customs Act* and is protected under the *Privacy Act*. The information will be used to make a determination of your application and may be shared with other government agencies in Canada and the United States of America. The information will be retained in the Personal Information Bank # CCRA PPU 042. Instructions for obtaining information are provided in Infosource which is available at public libraries, Government public reading rooms and on the Internet at: http://infosource.gc.ca.

FOR OFFICE USE ONLY

68.

☐ The applicant has paid the application processing fee.

CPC no.

FAST ID no.

SECTION F - FEE PAYMENT (non-refundable)

69. **The combined fee for an applicant to the FAST program is $80.00 Canadian or $50.00 U.S.**
All credit card fees will be processed as Canadian funds.

☐ I am enclosing a certified cheque or money order payment to the Receiver General For Canada ☐ Visa ☐ MasterCard

Card holder's name

Card no.

Expiry date ▶ MM YY

Card holder's signature

Printed in Canada

I-823F (10/02/2002) -- US Page 2